Romans Were Known For Their Aquaducks

And Other Gems of Wit and Wisdom in Western Civilization

℘ ℭ

Compiled & with Learned Notes

by

Brian E. Strayer, Ph.D.

SPYDERWORT PRESS
ALBANY, NY

For information, please contact Don Congdon Associates, Inc., 110 William St., Suite 2202, New York, NY 10038, USA. Email: dca@doncongdon.com

ISBN-13: 978-1502325136

ISBN-10: 1502325136

Cover image: Roman mosaic duck. Detail of Nilotic scene from the House of the Faun, Pompeii, 1st century C.E. Photo by Marie-Lan Nguyen. This photograph is in the public domain in those countries with a copyright term of life of the author plus 90 years or less.

Spyderwort Press
Albany, NY, USA

To
Dr. Floyd Greenleaf
and
Dr. Harry Leonard
Whose invitations to teach at
Southern Adventist University
and Newbold College
gave me the opportunity
to collect these gems

Foreword

When the host of Art Linkletter's "House Party" published his book *Kids Say the Darndest Things!* in 1957, he noted that small children often mix fantasy and reality, making their views of everyday life wildly askew. For twenty-five years, the crazy, zany, refreshing insights of kids on his weekly program amused us all. Isn't that *just* like children to say that, we all chuckled.

But years later, when these entertaining Baby Boomers and Generation Xers entered college, they were *still* mixing fantasy and reality, as the bloopers on their history and English essays demonstrated. Sometimes by viewing the past with twentieth-century expectations; by accepting television's distorted portrayal of history; by adroit misspellings, clever slips of the pen, or magnificent malapropisms, these youth produced a fractured, fictionalized, funny interpretation of key events and personalities.

As one who has taught history by the essay method at four colleges and universities, I have had a unique opportunity to read and collect hundreds of these bloopers straight from the pages of blue book exams. Some of these gems are witty; others show wise insights into human failures and foibles; while still others are hilarious mainly because of their ignorance of factual detail. It is this combination of the punny and the profound, the comic and the correct, the ribald and the rational which has led me to adopt the subtitle *Wit and Wisdom in Western Civilization.*

I wish to acknowledge the special assistance of my faithful readers Clark Bonilla, Alicia Homer, Theresa Jones-Darrough, Dave Sherman, John Love IV, and Jennifer Tremper in helping me spot, type, collate and keypunch these hundreds of witty gems for publication. Part of their remuneration has been the chuckles we've shared as we mined this raw ore from the quarries of student exams at the University of Iowa, Southern Adventist University, Newbold College, and Andrews University. If these bloopers prove nothing else, they demonstrate that Art Linkletter's "little kids" still say "the darndest things" when faced with college history exams!

In editing this collection of wit and wisdom, I have attempted to preserve the original wording—spelling, punctuation, and all—of each statement. In some cases, I have changed a verb tense or added a transitional word or phrase for smoother syntax, flow of wording, or identification. In the main, however, what you are about to read are witticisms uncut and unpolished, straight from the pens of freshmen and sophomores trying desperately to make some sense out of the past. Enjoy!

Brian E. Strayer
Professor of History
Andrews University
August 2014

Romans Were Known For
Their Aquaducks

1

The Hebrew God
Was As Old As Moses

Mesopotamia was begun by the Sumeritans. It is a small land area which today is found in Egypt off the Nile River. The Mesopotamians were comprised of Summarians and Babylonians. The Summarians lived between the Euphrates and the Tiger Rivers which flooded irregularly. They also had the River Nile which controlled their civilization.[1]

In Mesopotamia there were city-states between the Tiger and Euphrates River in 3000 B.C. Also there were articles written by using characters cut from stone and the building of Zuggrats, large stone buildings. One of the major contributions from the Mesopotamians was recording information on soft clay tablets in the shapes of livers and other parts of the body by reed-shaped styles. This was called cunative or cunniform writing. Soon, however, the Mesopotamians stopped using the pictogram and instead used cuneiform as their way of communication, which was like chicken scratches.

The Summarrians had many gods or dieties. Like most ancient civilizations, they were also polytheists (worshipping more than one god to cover themselves). One god was Ahura Mazda—the god of sun and light. Another was Ahurmia—the god of evil and darkness. A third was Nammu—the female creator of the universe. The religious concepts of the Summarians spilled over into western civilization. They and the Baby-lonians knew arithmetic and geometry and had sum understanding of algebra. The Mesopotamian culture used their mathematics, based on the

---

[1] Earlier on, the Egyptians controlled the Nile, but rivers, like civilizations, wandered in those days.

number 60, to build architectural structures like the Temple of Karnak.[2]

The Egyptians came up with a new form of writing called hyrogliphix or hygrogriphics, later refined as hyroglifics.[3] They contributed threw their great engineering feets. They designed the pyramids for their pharaoh's afterlife and built the Shinx, one type of pyramid, which was carved out of rock. (The pyramids are a range of mountains between France and Spain.) The Egyptians also had a well-organized math system (pie r2) and devised a solar calendar based on the cycles of the moon which was more effective than the lunar calendar.

They were also into medical advances such as mummification and practiced embalming. When their pharaohs were embombed,[4] they removed the blood and certain vital organs, filled them with special fluid, and rapped them. The storage containers they used to keep the body in were similar to today's caskets.

The body was placed in a tomb deep within the pyramid. Other rooms were filled with the everyday pleasures of life because it was believed that the spirit or Ka could come out of the body and wander the tomb. The pharaoh would use the games and instruments to entertain himself so he wouldn't be bored to death.

Socially, the Egyptians saw many changes. They excelled socially and were leaps and bounds beyond their counterparts. They gave us the hierercatical law code of Hammurabi, a Code of Ethics which stated simply, "An eye for an eye and a tooth for a tooth."

They also learned a great deal from the Hebrews and thus allowed their women to have a lot of freedom. There were major domos and chief concubines who were to entertain the dieties in dancing. It is evident that women were also priestesses, held administrative positions, and were the epidemi of lovelyness to their men. In royalty, women took part in the royal business. The Egyptians made them goddesses in major dieties such as Hathor and Thorth. Egyptian women had it good; they were everything.

Religion was a major influence in Egyptian culture. The Zirrugat, or stepped mound that surmounted the temple, was invented. Amenhotep IV said that everyone should worship the one god Anton. He was thinking

---

[2] The Temple of Karnak was built by the Mesopotamians but was sold and moved to Egypt to entomb the appropriate pharaoh.

[3] Little is known about hygrogriphics, but being a coastal civilization, the Egyptians undoubtedly used water-soluble ink in writing their hieroglyphics during this early era.

[4] The implications of the Egyptian belief in reincarnation did have "explosive" results on their culture.

correctly about their being only one god, but he got the wrong one. Egypt—what a place!

The Hebrews were common people. They were for the most part not high in the political seen. They became slaves to Egypt. But Moses led the Israelites from Jerusalem to Canaan between 1300 and 1200 B.C. When the Hebrews had escaped slavery in Egypt and were wandering in the desert and got thirsty and hungry, Jehovah provided them with water rather than soda pop.[5]

The Jews were unique in their Christianity. They were monotheistic while the other cultures around them were saturated with gods which were only different from humans in their power and in their immorality. The Hebrew God was as old as Moses. The Hebrew profits, who interpeded the Lord and his communications to the people, warned them that if they worshipped idols, Jahweh would be sure to punish them. They predicted that the Hebrews would allow the Jews to reestablish the temple in Jerusalem. These profits preached whatever they wanted to say, even if it displeased the authorities.

The Hebrew God, Yahwey, was not a diety who demanded ritual sacrifices without cause or meaning. The Jews had a very structed religion pointing towards a future event. The Bible was written to show the Israeli concept of spiritualism. The laws of the Hebrews were based mainly on moral behavior such as stealing, killing, and committing adultery.

They made a pact with God, a covenant that stated if they obeyed Him, He would care for and protect them. The other nations had no such insurance plan.

Women could be priestesses if they had been called by God. Their Pharisees were people who liked to show off their goodness by praying in synonyms.

The Hebrews became very warlike, an empirical people who had to change as empires grew. However, their God provided for the Hebrew poor. The nations around didn't. The southern kingdom of Judah was destroyed and taken hostage off to Babylon. Finally they returned to their homeland, and after 25 years, the State of Israel was established in 1948.

The Persians of Arabia were in the light from about 459 to 333 B.C. Arabia has many syphoons and very bad ones; it got into their hair even

---

[5] As professional complainers, the Hebrews at that stage would probably have set up a hue and cry for soda pop had they been aware of it.

with their mouths shut. Persia was divided into 20 providences. The Persians were notorious for their excleptic nature. They were of a more calm, almost sensual nature. Persian governors would keep pease with the native people and collect taxes.[6]

The Medo-Persians constructed the Suez Canal and created a good postal system. They also created the compass and gave us the I.R.S. Since they were Republicans, they created the federation, a unification of states under one in the eclecticism era, because they were mainly eclectic in their ways of being by themselves and all.

Around 250 A.D. the Persian Sassidans crossed into the Roman Empire by the Danube. Persia was to figure prominently in all of ancient history, eventually developing the Persian rug. They sponged up the culture and talents of a captive people into their own culture. They brought dance, were great partiers, and had lots of eating.

The Persians were also one of the first civilizations that began worshipping the myth gods. Their god Ahura Masdan was the god of good and Ahramada was the god of bad or evil. They also gave us the Ahura and the Zodiac, which is the zoo of the sky, where lions, goats and other animals go after they're dead.[7]

The Assyrians were a group to be afraid of; they were not like people, but came from a war-torn country. They were a warring tribe, extremely violent and forceful, who bothered everyone in the surrounding cities. They terrorized their opponents in war and often fought dirty.[8]

Their military machine inspired terror in the hearts of their subjects. They were brutal in seiging cities with gorilla warfare and slicing up people. They were cruel to their captors. Sacrificial babies and other dimented rituals dominated their lives. They were allowed to beat their wives under Solon's law.

The Assyrians developed the use of iron and the calvary to be used in war. This calvary was a deadly force. The Assyrians were the first ones to start a long-term army and the first to start and have a calvary. They literally steam rolled into Babylonia, Palestine, Persia, and Egypt.

Assyrian art was often gruesome, but it did show that they had some soft spot to them. They established a library at Nazareth. Their art forms

---

[6] This pastoral image of Persian governors dining on vegetables with their people before dunning them for taxes is an especially touching one.

[7] This idea of celestial immortality for pets pleased Persian children and should bring comfort to today's boys and girls who, reciting "Twinkle, twinkle, little star," need no longer "wonder what you are!"

[8] The Assyrians did bathe occasionally, however, but not as often as the Romans.

and winged creatures led to Christianity's angles. Their postal system was excellent—somewhat better than ours today.

The Zodiac is the zoo of the sky

The Chaldeans had all the seven wonders of the world. King Nebuchadnezzar of the Chaldeans built the hanging gardens for his wife who missed the mountains. That structure was hailed as one of the seven wonders of the world. At a height of 75 feet and a width of 400 square feet, it appeared to hang in midair from a distance.

The Hittites gave us a representative government. The Phoenicians used the cunei form of writing.[9] The gods of the Indians were chiefly Mahommad and Buddha. In their spare time they did lots of carving.[10]

Sad to say, these ancients disappeared, either through mixing with other cultures or dying off. But their legacy lives on. The civilizations of Mesopotamia, Egypt, Phoenicia, Assyria and Persia are what we know

[9] Here is another charming case of Sumerian cuneiform wandering northwards to Phoenicia. Explaining this cultural transference will doubtless provide fodder for future dissertations.

[10] Normally they carved in wood or ivory, but occasionally they carved up each other until the Crusaders arrived.

today as the "fertile crest." It is evident, therefore, that each of these kingdoms did give their own unique contributions and they are unique because they were so very different from one another.[11] All of these achievements started the ball of society rolling towards a better way of life.

The pyramids are mountains between France and Spain

---

[11] This profound insight would impress Aristotle centuries later—or was it earlier?

2

The Greeks Planted Colonists For Their Food Supplies

The Greeks started many trends and things which had more of a moral to them, such as eating with the proper utensils and word formations and the alphabet (some of it). They began to capitalize on the important things which was important to them, but we take them for granted (eating, washing, etc.). They were the ones who set the pattern and the other things that they did, and updated them somewhat. We as a whole today still live in their updated trends.

The Greeks were too thickly populated to be comfortable, so they planted colonists for their food supplies. The Greek city-states were Athens, Sparta, and Torah.

The Spartans were people who believed in the rough life. The democratic part of Sparta's government was the Assembly of Rome. The Spartans formed the Pellopensian League and the Athenians formed the Delta League.[12] The Spartans were able to dominate their neighboring city-states through the Penopennian League, although they had little navel power.[13]

Athens and Sparta became the big boys on the block. The many differences between them eventually led these two states into war with each of them pulling at victory. The only possible solution for peace seemed to be war. Sparta was to blame for the war with the Athenians,

---

[12] Thus the Athenians were off to a flying start with their Delta League.

[13] This weakness was later demonstrated when the Spartans turned belly up when Thebes conquered them.

because it built up this nice army and was just dying to try it out. This is quite similar to a kid with a new toy.

The helots revolted against Sparta and the Second Messianic War was on. War between Athens and Sparta was to be expected from such opposite city-states with opposite views on life, liberty and the pursuit of happiness. Probably the main reason for the differences of the Spartans and Athenians was because of their emphasis on different things.

Sparta built up this nice army and was just dying to try it out

The Athenians were very expressianistic. They admired the Spartans' bravery, but thought that talk and logic was a better way to solve problems. This was always a bone of contention between the two. Athens was a navel power and it was dependent on the trade for its economy. Athenians made coins attractive which made it easier to trade. After all, who wants an ugly coin?

The Athenians kept planting wheat and soon their fields' nutrients were depleted. So some guy took over and had them make olive and vine crops instead.

The Athenians built very elaborate temples and were ruled by what they wanted rather than by what was good for them. Pisistratus was the first dictator of Athens, although he did several good things such as promote religion, build new churches, and add public places.

In Athens, the highest social level was the free citizens who could be involved in politics. The next level was the surfs or helots. The final and lower level was the plain citizens. Neither the slaves in Athens nor the merits or women could vote. Greek free male citizens were allowed to vote but had to go to Rome to do so.[14]

The religion of the Greeks was mostly that of many gods. They worshipped in temples supported by different columns—Ionic, Doris,[15] and Corinthiena or Couthiance (which depicted leaves and other artistic realms of culture). Their religion was mostly that of occults. They also helped prepare the way for Christianity because they also built synogogues for places of worship.

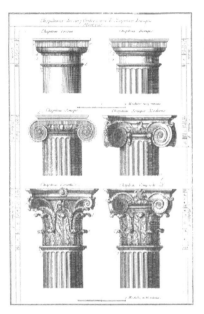

Ionic, Doris, and Couthiance orders

The Greeks worshipped twelve gods with Zues being the father of these gods. These were god-men, like superhuman powers, called anthroponology. Their gods were scandalous, immoral, and unsympathetic. So, with no example for them to follow, they turned to themselves to worship. Their religions, or religious cults, were an excuse for their festivals, dances, games, plays, etc.

---

[14] The Delta League flew citizens to Rome to vote, with package sightseeing tours including Naples, Ravenna, and the Riviera.

[15] Feminist art historians will welcome this revelation that one of the three famous Greek columns had a feminine origin.

℘ ℂ

Marriages back then were always arrayed in Ancient Greece. A dowry was set up and they wed. This was extremely unromantic.

Greek women had what is referred to as a sealed destiny: no choice or voice over their life or what happened to it. The men were free to go out and hold public offices, sleep with other women, generally to do as they pleased, while the women were expected to stay home to cook, sweep, clean, and take care of the household and husband. Their soul purpose in marriage was to bare heirs, especially male children, for the family and act as baby machines. This portrays what we call the double standard of modern society.

Greek women were not allowed to vote, take part in any public act, or own property. Only in instances where girls were born to the parent could a woman inherit property in Ancient Greece. Their home was at home. They had a specific place in the house called the gynocym, where they gathered to talk in the women's quarters, a special room in the back of the house (sometimes called the gymnastic[16]), which they were never to leave. The only function Greek women could do was the one of having children to maintain the human race, and cooking and waving. The family was raised by the mother till old enough for the father to take over at about ten.[17]

The only other way for women
to gain stature was by prostituition

---

[16] Greek women practiced aerobics in their gymnastics nearly every day.

[17] In those days, Greeks married while still very young.

But Greek women could participate in the religious life by being vestal virgins of the church. The only other way for women to gain stature was by prostituition as shown by Socrates' wife Aspiese.

Greek writing was more craftively created, more modern in form. In science, Ptolemy wrote on medicine and Gela wrote on astronomy. Both produced textbooks which were used into the sixteenth century. They must have been quite well bound to hold up that long.

Aristotle's ideas were written down in a handbook of sorts called the *Almagest* by Ptolemy. Elucid, a mathematician, made great theories in math with his hundreds of geometrical proofs. He developed the method of the hypothesis of a triangle which was equal. Euclid also wrote *The Complete Angler* because he knew all about angels.

Galen's theory that a child is born with a blank mind was very helpful in establishing the need for equal education of boys and girls. Today we also have followed the Greek idea of educating our young people in a similar (though different) manner.

When we look at the arts in this Greek period, we see an explosion of expression to succeed over negative forces. Drama came about first as a praise to Kynosis who was a god of wine and agriculture. Then Homer, who wrote the *Illot* and the *Oddessy*, felt that we should take credit for our own actions. His writings were a great form of hubris for himself. The two principal schools of philosophy were the Stoicis and the Etermanis.

Perhaps the young Greeks were among the first plastic surgeons. The physician Hirippodes found remedies. New human organs were also discovered. Veins and arteries were also able to be discovered.

The underlying principle of the entire Greek civilization was a search for perfection. This perfection had several characteristics: naturalness, order, and discipline. In this we can see movement towards the worship of the "holiness of beauty." The Greeks loved outward beauty more than inward beauty. They believed in the beauty of life.

In conclusion, the Greek philosophers studied and read and learned all they could from the past events and then started to formulate all these principles and facts which they had found into a little sermon which would lead into Christianity.

3

Alexander the Great
Was a Jock In His Time

Alexander was born to Darius III.[18] His father was killed while fighting the Persians because of what they did to his father. So Alexander took his father's place on the thorn.

His mother was also thought to be a relative of Achilles the Hun. Perhaps she was descended from that great warrior. Her own son inherited the Achilles tendencies.[19] He viewed himself as Acliess from Homer's poem "Iscess." He also said he was descended from Hercarees, one of the Greek gods. He was a great and mighty warrior with an exposed heel—his pride and drinking.

Pluto the Greek writer said of Alexander that he had a great thirst for learning. Aristotle taught Alexander the ways of the Romans, which he was fascinated with. He was smart, wrote poetry, and played both the lyric and the liar. He could do chariot jumping while the chariot was moving. He ordered his teacher Plato to commit suicide; then later in life, Alexander killed his tutor.

He became emperor of Rome after his father Philip died. One factor that made him a great leader was his ability to lead the armies of Rome. He first moved into Roman territory and conquered much land.[20]

---

[18] While this was not exactly an immaculate conception, it presents amazing new light on Alexander's origins.

[19] He was a well-heeled young man.

[20] This amazing ability of the Ancients to roam about, appearing where least expected, is shown by Alexander's remarkable career.

Alexander's personality was charming and even bewitching. He was a great outdoors man, a jock in his time. He killed a lion with his bare hands. At age twelve, he was the only one that could train a white-winged horse, Bucephalus. Alexander was often envied by his men because of such qualities of being a jock, outdoors man, and expert horseman.

For the women of his time, he was probably what we today would call a hunk. He loved to play the harp and have sex, although he never committed adultery.[21] He was a very strange individual. He never used to take baths. His temper was a definite rage. He was one of those people that could sell Eskimos refrigerators.

He loved Eastern women, so he married a few of them. He married Satire, the daughter of Darius III, and also the daughter of Arteczurchies. His sexual virtues were astounding. He married every woman he had sexual relations with and he encouraged his soldiers to do the same.

These Hellenistic women still had to rely on the man's world. Most of them were treated as prostitutes. Some were treated as a trade or business. Others had it a little easier: they were just male companions. Alexander watched what he ate so as not to become weak from food poisoning or to become fat.

At the death of Corinth, he was voted to be general. He got 30,000 Bermins and trained them and sent them back to Greece for later use. Before battles, he was superstitious and made human sacrifices. A great military strategist, he was able to motivate his troops and he never won a battle.[22] He never raped women because of losing a battle, however. His army was not only strong in military ways, but was also strong in spirit. He was their leader and they idolized him. His men had it all together. He gave the Roman spirit a shot in the arm.

Alexander was a trend setter. He shaved his beard and had his men follow suit, since he believed that would be helpful in battle. The enemy would not be able to grab the beard to hold the man as he ran a spear through him or removed his head. Soldiers should, after all, have clean beards when they go to war because that won't hinder their fighting.

Alexander went beyond his principle of moderate drinking and drank too many Hercules. He drank from the Herculean cup which contained six ounces of wine, which he consumed with no problem. One of his vices was alcohol. He drank eight gallons of it during one contest to see who could drink the most wine, then consumed three gallons or one talent at another feast. He could drink six quarts at one meal without batting an

---

[21] This high standard of morality challenges harpists even today.

[22] This highlights the importance of motivation, especially if one is going to lose every time.

eye, although he usually drank three quarts of wine with one meal. He could also drain the goblet of Hercules containing six gallons.[23]

He held drinking contests so that everyone else would feel as awful as he felt afterwards. He picked up what we know today as malaria, which bothered him every once in awhile.

In 331 B.C. Darius III was king of a vast Persian empire. But he knew what to expect. By 332 B.C., Alexander was chasing him down. Darius noticed that Alexander was leading a fleet into victory and felt that they must be stopped immediately. Darius had a large army which confronted Alexander at the Battle of Issus in 333 B.C. Alexander should be called "the great" because with his army of 35,000 men he defeated the Persian army of 1000 men. He would be right in the mist of fighting. He was undefeated in battle. But by the time Alexander's soldiers arrived home, many of them had lost their lives.

Alexander conquered almost the eastern western part of the world. He also controlled Palestine, Egypt, and Symaria. He made many great strives forward for Rome. But he had no use for Christians and started to persecute them. He had Paul beheaded and Peter crucified.

Alexander never lost a battle, except for the one at the very end. That was the battle between him and death. Death won, for he finally died cold, out of his conceited, intemperamental soul at the age of 33 on June 13, 1923.[24] He was the same age as one other great person who died at 33—God.

He became a loser because of his low value for life which caused his death. Alex had a lot going for him: brains, courage, swiftness, influence, and good looks. Too bad he blew it all away. What does it profit a man to gain the whole world yet lose his sole.[25]

But you don't get smoke without some fire, so apparently people saw Alexander as very great. The Fertile Crescent became a symbol of the Greek Empire. Alexander will never be forgotten for expanding Rome and helping to make the Roman Republic a great one. He built some 700 cities, and was a strong believer in the electric approach—mixing different cultures. Science really boomed during the Hellenistic period.

Alexander succeeded in unifying both his military and the fast Roman Empire. He established German colonies everywhere, not only

---

[23] Perhaps some future Bartenders Union convention can clear up this discrepancy concerning the capacity of the Hercules Cup.

[24] Because of all his drinking, Alexander was a remarkably well-preserved man.

[25] That long trek back from India was very hard on the sandals.

conquering Egypt but places far away from his home—India (now Iran), North Africa, and England.[26] It was at the Passage of Hercules (now known as the Passage of Gibraltar) where Alexander lost his first and only battle—the Battle of Nice.

In Egypt they thought Alexander was the son of their god Emma. The Greeks believed him to be the son of Zeses. Even the stubborn, hard-headed Romans finally accepted him as divine, although the Greeks were more on the philosophy side while the Romans were law and order types.

Alexander never lost a battle, except for the battle between him and death

The Hellenistic Greek philosophers after Alexander aided in the preparation of the Christian era because they taught that there was a universal law in which to live by, that considered everyone as brothers and sisters who belonged to a family determined to reach a certain goal—

---

[26] It is unfortunate that Alexander's conquests of Rome, Germany and England have been almost totally forgotten today. Much more research needs to be done on Hellenistic influences in these regions.

to live by the law of their God. Hellenistic philosophers gave way to Christian theology because of their belief in both an evil god and also a religious god. Thus the Greeks and Christians differed yet they were the same. It seems that the ideas are close, but not really. The Christians are in a class by themselves and they did not follow any other cultures so to speak.[27]

Alexander played both the lyric and the liar

---

[27] The exact manner in which Christianity resembled Hellenistic ideas is here a little bit muddled, so to speak.

4

The Romans Were Known For Their Aquaducks

The legendary founders of Rome were Romulus and Rommel.[28] Under the Roman Republic, Marius and Sulla were elected to be the next leaders. They got jealous of each other. Marius was elected consul, then his term ended and Sulla was elected. Marius took it away from Sulla by popular and equestrian support. Sulla said, No way; I won't have that! So he took his forces and went in and took back his office of consul.

The Romans had a system of give and take. They provided citizenship as a carrot to the people of the republic. This tended to unify them. But the inflation was so high that there were only two main classes of people: the plebians who were the poor farmers and the parisians who were wealthy landowners.

The patriarchs were the upper class. Soon social conflict broke out between two other groups: the omptical and the popular. The poor pheasant farmers couldn't pay their taxes, so they joined their land to wealthy landlords and worked for them.[29] Small farms were merged with other small farms to form co-ops. The Romans' chief industry was agriculture. The economy helped to unify the lower class and keep them quiet because there wasn't much they could say with their mouths full of grain.

---

[28] This fact, germane to Roman history, is often overlooked. Rommel was a good friend of Alexander the Great who, you may recall, died in 1923.

[29] These pheasant laborers, who first make their appearance in Ancient Rome, proved to be a remarkably enduring class throughout the Middle Ages, as subsequent chapters will reveal.

More currency was on the market, which raised prices and caused people to spend money like women.

During the first and second techiruss or triumvirate, the people were all holding their breath to see which of the three rulers would be on top. Ten years later, Gaius Gracchus, Tiberius' younger brother, got himself elected emperor while Caesar was fighting Gouls in Gaul, the southeastern part of the empire.[30] (The modern name for Gaul is Vinegar.)

Julius Caesar was eventually killed in a battle there in 53 BC. The Roman Republic then collapsed slowly due to several factors. For one, three emperors tried to rule the land with their wealth, military expertise, and knowledge. But three's a crowd.

Three's a crowd

---

[30] Julius Caesar, too busy chasing ghosts in Gaul, fails to mention in his chronicles this brief imperial rule by Gaius Gracchus, which suggests the need for a revisionist history of Octavian's later reign.

The last major step in the Republic's dissolving was the continued overthrow and disposal of leaders. In 204 BC Scilio led the army and reconquered the Italian cities. In 202 BC at the Battle of Zama he defeated Hannibal. Rome eventually became a democracy. Phili of Preene received the political office of majestrate, during which she paid or funded the aquaducks and resivwars. In Rome at that time there were women libbers fighting the new Appian Law.

Under the Roman Empire, Augustus also delegated authority, as Jethro suggested Moses do. He had complete control over the army as well as the government by his hand-in-the-glove friendship with Agrippa. For awhile, there was one loony emperor after another. One out of fifteen emperors survived a violent death.

Octavius finally made it to the top. At a very young age he later became known as Nero. When Nero grew older, he succeeded his mother and had her put to death along with Seleneca, his own tutor. He was meotic and unconcerned about the welfare of his people. Emperors like Nero were a little on the whacko side. Nero was known to be very free sexually. He had no morals in Christian standards and felt free to explore sex with more than one person.

Perhaps Nero is most famous for his alleged involvement in the Circus Maximus fire in 64 AD which destroyed four provinces and badly damaged six others.[31] He burned the Roman Empire for background for his poetry recital. He then had the gall to blame the great fire on the Christians. He dipped them in grease and burned them at the stack. He covered them with wax and set them alight to illuminate the city. Flaming Chrisians were the main attraction at Nero's garden orgies. He also had big-man Christian Paul killed. Later Diocletian burned Rome and tried to blame the Christians as well.

Emperor Caligula, being a mean sort of person, had problems in that he often engaged in whimsical cruelty. Diathelis was one of the toughest emperors. In 303 AD he destroyed books and churches for the wealth and land, kicked Christians out of office, took their money, fined them heavily, tortured and killed thousands. Antoninus Pius, on the other hand, had such a peaceable time that there was nothing to write about by historians. Everything was hunky-dory.[32]

St. Augustine was another emperor. But toward the end of the empire, emperors came and went like flies on a carcass. Constantine took over in the West and in 324 AD became the soul ruler.

---

[31] The extent of the Circus Maximus fire helped to popularize the word "maximum" among Roman insurance adjustors, implying total loss.

[32] This era is often called "the dog days" of the Empire.

The Romans had a good loyal army which was controlled by consoles.[33] Roman manipals consisted of 120 men. The next largest formation consisted of 360 men, then the century of 1000 men and the legion of 3600 men. The army was the right arm of the government. This army was very stern; all the soldiers meant business. It was unreal. They were able to be tolerant so as to bend but not to break. It was healthy to be on the Romans' side.

It was healthy to be on the Romans' side

The military was definitely strengthened by uniting into one main army answerable to the emperor and loyal to him rather than several armies loyal only to the general, running off whenever the grass was greener somewhere else. Many of the soldiers fighting for Rome were not Romans but Italians who were not as loyal. The soldiers' retirement plan was in good shape, however. They had veterans' colonies with a retreaded general to stay there which kept an uprising from occurring.

When the army conquered someone, the providence was almost able to carry on as normal. But when the empire started getting bigger, the generals by this time had such big heads that they were killing one another and the men underneath them realized that that wasn't going to work. Many of the soldiers started to put their trust in the leader of the

---

[33] To hear these consoles, or quadrophones, sounding off while marching was a real stereophonic experience. Today's "squadron" is derived from the Roman quadrophone.

military expedition—men such as Napoleon. Roman military expenses were running high and were making the money they had run very thin and scarce.

The Romans were also electric, very cosmopolitan in respect to culture. While maintaining a unique system of law and military, they adopted Greek art, philosophy, and academic traditions. Thus captive Greece took its captor captive.

The writers of the time wrote about history and politics instead of love. The Romans were athletic and combative. The Greeks, on the other hand, were intellectual and philosophical. Given an arena, the Greeks would debate and the Romans would cheer on a gladiatorial duel.

Romans sculpted men as they actually looked, with ugly noses, fuzzy hair, and weak chins. Roman plays were different from the Greeks in that they were more dramatic, filled with much more harsh violence. Their law and architecture expressed their desire for order. Their government was a quick government. The religious cults, the Cynics, Epicureans, and Celtics,[34] were borrowed from the Greeks.

In their architecture, they started a style called the imperial style which brought in the bathhouses, temples, and arenas. The Romans were known for their aquaducks[35] and the running of cold, fresh water into Rome through those bridge-like dudes.

The Roman army was also a superb construction contractor. Rome had an A-1 system of roads, excellent, faster, more fantastic than anyone else's. They were wide and smooth, very plush for their time. The roads were like spokes of a wheel which helped to make the wheel stronger. The Romans also had a good taxi system. Mail was delivered faster in northern England in Roman times than it is now.[36] In this way, when the different ambassadors came to Rome for conference meetings, the empire could make rules and judgments more clearly because of the ambassadors' firsthand knowledge.

The Romans had plumbing, sewers, and they even took baths. They built theaters, palaces, collusiums, and other buildings. The Roman

---

[34] Today in Boston this strange religious rite, with round balls and metal hoops, draws thousands of devout Hellenes to worship at the Celtic temples.

[35] Rubber duckies were especially popular in the public baths, where the therapeutic effects of a dip in the caldarium with one's aqua duck floating nearby can scarcely be imagined today.

[36] The Labour Party should take note of this fact and see what can be done to speed the postal chariots today.

sewage disposal system kept the city clean (why it's a dirty place today is not known). All of these factors glued the empire together.

The Romans also contributed cathedrals more elaborate than the Greeks, and had their own distinct form of government, which they didn't eclect from Greece. In conclusion, Greece and Rome were alike, but not really; Rome only looks like Greece.

The Romans called the father's authority the *patria potestas*, which in literal terms means "do what you will." Males were the dominant man in the household in the Ancient World. But unlike the woman-dominating Greeks, Roman women had a little more going for them. They were more than just property, more than just the managers of the household, more than produce machines. They were women of Rome who were more free to roam around. They could leave their homes and go out into their communities to shop at the market and go to the theater and church, whereas in Greece, men only went to church and came back and shared that with the family.

The respectable woman wore the stoga. Under the empire, equality began to be built up for women. There was a system in which slave girls were registered prostitutes. In this way, the men who wanted sex would do so with these women rather than with other men's wives, thus keeping everyone happy.[37]

Romans invented contraceptives like the condom from a goat bladder. This resulted in less babies and more sex, but more importantly, the increase of childless marriages. Bachelors were taxed a special tax to attempt to prompt them into marriage. By mid-century women's status was starting to change to sine manu, without control, by which the father kept his control until his death. Once a woman had three children she could divorce her husband. But the husband had the right to have an affair, especially when the woman could not bare children. The Vestal Virgins, however, were to remain celibate and act as the nuns of their day.

The Romans did not like the uprisings that Jesus stirred up. They persecuted Jesus and hoped the Jews would forget Him, but they didn't. They kept right on preaching and talking about Him. Christians who never conformed to the demands of rulers were a great worm of the empire.

---

[37] Although if everyone were so happy, why aren't more of those old Roman busts and statues smiling?

An important aspect to note is that the Christians did not want to pay the taxes to support the Roman government. So Nero and others did cruel things like burning them, which did not go over well with the Christians.

Some were persecuted because they were very wealthy and the Romans wished to have their riches. Roman authorities made it a businesslike procedure to attend chapels and fake gods' meetings and anybody that didn't like it would turn out on the next lion's menu. Persecuting Christianity was like trying to stamp out flaming gasoline— the more you try to stamp it out, the more it spreads.

*Anybody that didn't like it would
turn out on the next lion's menu*

The Christian church formed a sisterhood for women that enabled them to find themselves. Christians and those who rebelled would be seen at the next coliseum event as food for the lions. But Christianity had a huge impact on Rome. Later, Constantine had his army carry Bibles to their next battle.

The empire gained unity through its economy by making Roman coinage the universal currency. But because of the attitude and lack of interest, other cultures that were left alone to brood on Roman dominance rose to power and plotted coops which were well planned attacks that were started by generals who wanted to destroy someone who was in charge.

The seeds of decay were present long before 476 AD. As the government rocked and tittered, the people were crushed. Basically it seems as though the Roman Empire was living off past profit—but all this was slowly running out. Rome declined due to the frightening inflation of the dollar and to assignations and plots towards the emperor.[38] Roman rulers were killed off like pigs in a barn.

It was a doggy-dog world. Military coos came and went like the weather, with power changing hands faster than students' money does. Yet the people in Rome went on galavanting throughout and seemed to be hedonistic. The fall of Rome was like a mighty chain that link by link went to pieces until it got to the ball on the end, which happened to be the continual barbaric invasions.

The barbarians, such as the Huns, Ostrogoths, Visigoths, Vandals, Saxons, Germans, and Anglos, did the worst thing for Rome by taking over the frontiers. The last to ransack Rome was Attica, a member of the Goths. The Huns under their King Atila, or "the scourge of God," snowballed into the empire, forming themselves into avdummerers and crossing the steppes of Russia. They were very cruel and hardy.

The empire gradually declined because on the eastern border, Rome was being invaded by a new dynated called the Old Persia turned new. The Sassaids plundered providences in the east as the Goths reached the Balkans and built a pirate fleet to disrupt trade in the Mediterranean. Meanwhile, the Vandals drove from northern Germany into Spain, then into South Africa.[39] Then the Vandals sacked Rome in 455 AD. Poor Rome!

All these factors worked like acid on clothing to deteriorate the Roman Empire. Rome decayed and collapsed into a hopeless heap, decaying as corrosion in aircraft, rust on nails, and erosion of the soil.

So the empire declined because of some bad trouble in their community. During the reign of ruling, things had been going bad because citizens were passive and apathied. The whole Roman Empire had to decline, however, or something worse could have happened and that would have been a bad mistake.[40]

---

[38] While the denarius wasn't in very good shape, the dollar inflated much worse, so that emperors got fewer assignations for their money.

[39] Unlike other barbarian tribes who only walked or snowballed, the Vandals' ability to drive helps explain their rapid expansion, even into South Africa.

[40] Here we have a fine example of positive determinism.

5

Charlemagne Was an All-American Hero

The barbarians, as their name implies, weren't very intellectual. Their way of life seemed pretty primitive and stupid. The two races living in the north of Europe were the Esquimax and the Archangels. In their language, they were Romans. The barbarian tribes adopted Roman armor such as the helmet or sepulchar.[41]

In religion, we find many symbols of Christianity. There are many pictures of angles with orbs in their hands and wings, which is very Christian. Other religious symbols included the cross and the orb, symbol of world dominion which can be seen on the top of King Abiligulf's crown. Their Catholic Mess was written in Latin, which is very difficult.

Monasteries and convents sprang up everywhere like freshly sown grass on good earth. Monks and nuns both contributed in the establishment of monarchies in the wilderness. St. Anthony gave away 300 acres and moved into the desert. He was the father of eremitica monasticism which was the belief to give up everything to go into the desert to live a life in solitude. There were so many followers of his that they weren't in solitude anymore.

The Cisterines were a branch of monks who used their money and position to develop better plows, better ways of using the land, and better irritation techniques. One of St. Patrick's followers, Augustus, brought his message to England which began at Canterbury. But even though the

---

[41] Sepulchars, as the name implies, were lightweight disposable caskets so that in case a warrior got killed, he could more easily be buried on the spot.

Roman Catholic Church made significant contributions to the Early Middle Ages, things weren't all peaches and cream.

A lot of kings were only joining the church for secular reasons, to win battles. It took a long time to sink from their heads to their hearts. These sixth century barbarian cultures show Christian influence in the eye-for-an-eye and tooth-type of law where families carried out their own justice; it was not left up to the state to decide. They may have gotten this from the old law of Moses. Their concept of law was ordeals, consorpation, weregeld, and if anything else failed, a blood bath.[42]

They also had a funny trial system, for the barbarians were accustomed to innocence only when the guilt was proven. They also had courts as did the Romans, but these were very different. To see if someone was guilty, they would throw them in a pond: if they sank, they were innocent, but if they floated to the top, they were guilty.

The big difference was the way they made wrongs right. They believed in the eye-for-an-eye policy. Their Saline Law stated that you must take everything with a grain of salt. The family was usually involved in some way. If a man was killed, then the family would kill the killer to even the score. All in all, the Germans were still semi-barbarians but more civilized about it.

The Germans were still semi-barbarians but more civilized about it

In Galatia, the Celtics were taught by Paul in the first century and later moved to Ireland. These Christian Celtics taught that December wasn't the birth of Christ and they taught people how to survive. The

---

[42] Since the barbarians hated taking baths, the blood bath was a particularly effective deterrent to crime.

Welsh Celtics held out for quite awhile.[43] Dinooth of Wales had an ally who was King Arthur. The king told everyone to listen to Dinooth or suffer the vengeance of death.

At age 16, Patrick was captured by parrots and sold into slavery in Ireland. He changed the Itala Bible version into a language that the people could not understand. Both Patrick and Columba had been against the authority of the pope, so it is quite ironic that they were both maid saints. Columba, a student of St. Patrick, was leader of the Columbines of Scotland. Columbanus, who was somewhat like the Johnny Appleseed of his day, spent time clearing forests and planting gardens while he preached the word of God. In God's name he witnessed in France, spreading the truth until Queen Broomhilda got mad and forced him out of Australia and he went immediately to Austria.[44]

In France, Clovis was king of what was called the Meraigiagiai Dynasty. He fought a battle against the Alumni in 506 AD.[45] His turn to Catholic Christianity in 500 AD marked a significant turning point for the German people. He declared that he could no longer stand heretics living near him. He then used his religion as an excuse to drive out the Vistagoth heretics.

Pepin the Short was the next ruler of France who took over from the Mayerlums. He was crowned king by Boniface and was anointed by Pope Zacharist I. Then Pippine became mayor of Austria and Nestoria. Pope Stephen II gave Pippine several titles: Romeus Petracus (which means he was saved), Patrich Romansorum, and Popicius Romanicius. Pippine attacked the Lombards in Italy and gave the pope more breathing room.

Charlemagne was the President of France.[46] On Christmas day in 800 AD Pope George II crowned Charlemagne Emperor of Rome. Charlemagne started the CIA[47] or the *messi demenici*, in an attempt to stop the counts' growing power. Once a year, these envoys monitored the counts. Then Charlemagne annexed the French side of the mountains for France. This united all of Goth.

---

[43] In the twentieth century, however, an enticing offer from Boston persuaded them to move to the U.S.

[44] Because of continental drift, Australia and Austria were much closer in proximity in those days.

[45] Mainly because the Frankish graduates refused to support the proposed endowment fund at Paris.

[46] Frankly speaking, this early attempt at establishing a French Republic has been ignored by scholars.

[47] The Charlemagne Intelligence Agency.

Along with Pippin, he headed the Germanic invasion which drove the Lombards out of Spain. He was playing a role like a decathlon winner, getting over and around obstacles that stood in his way and also making improvements as he went along on his course. He was like the conductor of an orchestra: he put everything together. He played the role of a knight in shining armor; he was the cowboy with the white hat.

He helped repulsate France in education. The Carolingian renaissance taught Christian and classical principles and philosophies to the pheasants.[48] Charlemagne also put the icing on the cake when he made tithing compulsory.

Simon de Montfort challenged Charlemagne's authority. Then Charlemagne's three sons killed him. After his death, the land was split into three parts. Charles the Bald got France, Lather had the imperial crown and Italy, and Louis had Germany. All in all, Charlemagne was an all-American hero, but he wasn't born in America.[49] But if he had been, it would have been great for our morale; we really need the boost.

Then Boniface went to Frankland to convert the still heathen Germans, the Faisons in Saxony. He helped unify a Christian kingdom in France. He also established monasteries in Monte Casino. Roshwita studied and wrote poetry, novels, plays, and narratives. She was just one example of the educated empresses of the Byzantine period. Eleanor of Aquitaine supported chivalry because it was known as the Romantic Age. The Carolingian code was monogamy, but they practiced polygamy instead.

Greg the Great was king of the kingdom of Anglo-Saxon England. The king used a counsel known as the Y-tan. The kings also brought the organized Roman Church to the Anglo-Saxons which made them more moral. As long as one was faithful and loyal and peace was in the air, one could walk in the towns with a sack of gold and no one would torment him.

Basically, the Anglo-Saxons were nice guys. They divided their lands into cheers and counties and were loyal to the main government. Some land was divided into shires and ruled by shire-eves.[50] The common people had more freedom and there was less feuding because the land

---

[48] Unlike today's ring-necked pheasant, which has a very low IQ, the Medieval pheasants were the most intelligent birds served up on the counts' tables at dinner time.

[49] The possibility of early Carolingian voyages of exploration to America—possibly to the Carolinas—needs further investigation.

[50] These "Eves," or female administrative officials, have long been overlooked in studies of Anglo-Saxon local government.

was not feudalized like it was later under the Normans. They divided their courts into reeves with a shire in control.

Otto the great started the Ottoman Empire. As Emperor, he brought the rebirth. During this tenth century renaissance, Gerber was one of the most influential churchmen of the time and eventually became pope.[51] The Roman Church was in need of his reforms because of its clinical marriage and simony beliefs in the eleventh century. Clinical marriage was deemed unlawful and unwise. The domination of lay people over the papacy led to secularization or a decline in spiritualism in the church.

When William of Normandy was named by Edward the Confessor as heir to his throne, this ticked off Early Harold, who was becoming a very strong force in England. But William faced little opposition because the lords and barons didn't bother with Harold much any ways.

When the Normans invaded England in 1060 AD, King Edward I and his army had just finished pushing back the Northmen or Vikings. These Vikings or Mormons were barbarians from Scandinavia, great horsemen from the East, and Muslims from the South. They had played a big part in the collapse of Charlemagne's empire. As Harold in 1066[52] was crossing the Thames River, he fell off his horse and drowned. William then marched on Paris and was excepted as king. Then England was invaded by Catholicism under Henry V. The ensuing Battle of Hastings brought about the landing of the Normans and Angol-Saxons.

The Norman fighting technique was the calavary, which gave them quicker mobility. The Normans made effective use of this calavary which quickly disposed of the Anglo-Saxon way of fighting. William I immediately seized all the lords' land and futilized it.

The Norman king had full control of his government; his say was *the* say. William I used torture and even death to bring about obedience. He then introduced feudalism which he and his airs that followed him strengthened. Their system, which resembled fugal government, and their legal system, not only was of great benefit to England, but it presented certain principles that have been carried through in some form to society today.[53]

The Normans had a doorstep justice system. This meant that one was to get a fair shake in the trial. Also they had certain taxes such as the

---

[51] Because of advances in nutrition at this time, Gerber grew to rotund dimensions and enlarged the papal throne.

[52] The different calendars used by the Anglo-Saxons and the Normans account for this six-year discrepancy from 1060 to 1066 AD.

[53] This fugal government harmonized Mormon feudal practices with Anglo-Saxon models of jurisprudence.

Dansfield Tax. William I sent out his *missi dominici* into the country to collect the journals of the landholders. The Normans had no time for writing. The peasants became surfs under Norman rule.[54]

William I was drowned in a butt of Malmsley wine; he never laughed again. After he died in 1807, Rufus, his son, took over his throne. Then King Henry I sent out delegates more often and used them to replace shire reefs as judges.[55] But Henry I was lazier than William I, so he sent out the royal envoys so often that the judges became circuit judges known as justices of ire. They tried cases concerning the king's vessels. The Normans under Richard the Conqueror then declared that all belonged to the king.

Henry II improved England's system of taxation by getting people to collect and record the taxes. These people were called sherrifs, barons, and clerks. They were a simpler version of the IRS. His minister, Thomas a Becket, put on a camel hair shirt and his life at once became dangerous. Finally, Edward II came to the throne.

Becket's life at once became dangerous

Feudalism and manorialism had a sweet side and a sour side. Feudalism promoted community pooling of efforts. The king was the highest in rank which had lords and vessels underneath. He owned all the land and had

---

[54] Since no spot in England is more than 50 miles from a large body of water, surfing and other water sports caught on rapidly.

[55] Highly trained legal experts, the shire reefs were also adept at surfing and reef snorkling.

workers put on it to care for it. This made a lot more surfs, but it didn't permit the lords to overpower the king with excess wealth. The king even went to extremes to execute his reign. He had a court called the Wynat which collected debts, advised the king, and balanced the treasury.[56]

The lords were the head honchos, so to speak. The lord lived in the manor, or the Main House, similar to the White House. The demesne was the lord's land, the land he used for whatever. Aristocratic nobility included the Knits.[57] Noblemen were the queens, princes, and wives of dukes, nights, barons, etc. For entertainment, the noblewomen went to the mock battles put on by the pheasants and surfs.

Aristocratic nobility included the Knits

The vassal knights were a fine protection agency for the people and lords. The land and rights owned by a vassal were called benefices at first, later fifes. Vassals benefited most from feudalism because they received

---

[56] The Wynat derived from Henry II's typical response when new taxes were proposed: "Why not?"

[57] These Knits originated in Scotland, where from time immoral, they had knitted colorful tartans for the highland clans. The wisest among them were respectfully called "Knitwits."

protection, a fief, and had time to socialize. The vassals led pretty happy and fulfilled lives. These knights evolved from being Pittsburgh Steelers into ballet dancers over time.

The pheasants labored, the lords provided protection, the knights fought and enforced law, and the clergy watched over the lord's sheep. The pheasant was also required to give advice to his lord if he was asked, and also to sit as a member of his lord's council. Freedmen became surfs. Having to do the same work as their father created basic moral problems of those more free-spirited surfs.

One disadvantage was that striking pheasants could ruin the system. The pheasants' crops were also often destroyed by the nobles' running their chariots through the gardens.[58] Pheasants rebelled against their lord for this, but they were unsuccessful. But the fact that they rebelled showed that things were not going foot loose and fancy free. The pheasants' revolting also was a cause for the Protestant Reform. The weekend Holy Roman Empire was another cause.[59]

Feudalism was like living in a world of survival. Most of the surfs and pheasants needed insurance and security. But no matter what class one was in, there was always food on the table (though it probably wasn't roast beef) and clothes on one's back (though they were probably not from Sax Fifth Avenue in New York).

The crusaders were a wild and savage people. The peasants on crusade were led by Peter the Hermit and William the Penniless who preached to them and took to marching on to the Holy Lands. The peasants, who already thought they were hell bound, jumped at the opportunity to change that. Thus came the peasant crusade or Crusade #1, which was the best example of the Holy Push.

If one were killed on crusade, one's sins were all instantly forgiven and he went to heaven on the fast train with a ticket to the Eternal Life Station. Even the knights could not resist the temptation of a pure sole from God during the crusades.[60] If he was not fortunate enough to be killed, while he was gone at least, he was exempt from all taxation on

---

[58] While knights normally rode horses, occasionally, after imbibing too much mead, they went on wild chariot rides through the countryside.

[59] The Holy Roman Empire was such a vast territory that the emperor governed it effectively only on the weekends, when he perambulated with his justices and held court.

[60] To be sure, the long trek from France to Palestine wore out a good many impure soles.

debts and property back home. People went on crusades for God, Glory, and Gold. Crusaders battled in common for the glory of God, country, and pocketbook.

Pope Urban II promised the people of Europe that their sins would be forgiven on the condition that they would join the church. The pope wanted to unite all religions under the Roman Catholic Church.

The crusades also occurred because Emperor Alexus picked a fight with the Seljuks, and after being roundly spanked by the aforementioned Turks, he called on Pope Urban II to send him money. Urban II was a very powerful pope, and with that, he began to think that, well, if I come up with a concept that will drive people to war, why not do it? So he came up with the idea of fighting in the holy crusade so one is guaranteed a ticket to heaven. Then Emperor Alexus asked Pope Leo IX for help. Neither Patriarch Michael Cerularius from the East nor Leo IX came prepared to negotiate. Both leaders ended up extraditing the other.

On the first crusade, four leaders headed it: Raymond of Saint Gillus, Godfrey of Buillon, Duke of Lorei Baldwin, and Bohemon of Toronto.[61] These were men who enjoyed adventure and fighting; some were already fighting amongst themselves. Then when offered a chance to go and serve their country and fight and still gain salvation—what a deal!

Not only that, but they had the likely chances of gaining wealth, status, maybe even a title. Not many wanted to pass it up. Knights were urged on to recapture the Holy Land from the infidels and to kill a Turk for Christ. People responded and continued the cascade of crusades because there was political and papal support for them.

But when the Muslims built up their energies again, this led to the third crusade. This crusade of the kings included Richard I (Lionhearted) of England, Emperor Frederick Barbossa of Germany, and Phillip II Augustine of France.

The Turks committed atrocities against Christians (i.e., removing their entrails, forcing them to walk and pull the entrails out, seeing if they could cut their heads off with one sword swipe). King Augustine of France drowned to death coming back from the third crusade and Richard the Lion Heart of England was captured by Germans and put in prison in Austria where he was handsomely ransomed.

The fourth crusade was called by Innocent III, who was anything but innocent. It was launched by the papacy for dominance over the Europeans. Crusaders were distracted to destroy Zara to provide a

---

[61] That some knights came from Canada demonstrates that recruitment among the nobility was much more widespread geographically than scholars once thought.

passage way to Palestine for the Phoenicians.[62] The church believed that if they could convert more souls, they would gain increasing power. Never mind that they would be converting at knife point.

The fifth, sixth, and seventh crusades were small. At least the textbooks don't expand too much on them.

The crusades had some positive effects through all this mess. One thing is that the language began to break down. Trade flourished with silk dyes and swell cotton cloth was introduced. Baths with bubbles came into play. The crusades introduced guitars and flamingo dancing.[63]

One negative effect of the crusades was the lack of intolerance towards other religions. Meanwhile in Spain, the Inquisition was moving along rather nicely. Jews, Muslims, Gypsies, and heretics were being tortured to death left and right.

The Inquisition was moving along rather nicely

---

[62] The Phoenicians were the naval cowboys of the Ancient and Medieval world, perpetually wandering, searching for the lost vowels in their alphabet.

[63] When brought to the New World, flamingo dancing became wildly popular in Spanish Florida.

6

A Buttress Is the Wife of a Butler

Perhaps what is seen in the twelfth century is not so much an outpouring of energy as it is a shift in energy. Man was becoming more civilized. Instead of using energy to fight each other, they used the energy to expand trade, express their thoughts and feelings in stories, poems, and worship to God in the glory of their architecture.

Banking was becoming very popular. Bankers weren't, but banking was. So merchants expanded trade routes to the Far East in which they could secure a greater prophet.[64] After all, money is only money if one believes in it. People began to produce more, travel more, and this brought about a dissatisfaction with what they had. They wanted what Joe over in Tenbucktwo had and began to trade with him for something he wanted. Soon, however, Western Europe had reached a limit of food production and manufacturing because of so-so soil and limited technology.

During the twelfth century also, universities popped up everywhere (though not like weeds) to replace monastic schools where education was very limited, since one could only study to be a bishop or abbot, maybe a pope. These early cathedral schools were organized into chapters and run by cannons, who were priests or candidates for priesthood.[65]

Universities were widespread throughout Europe and especially

---

[64] This search for a great prophet eventually led to the crusade to find Prester John, as chapter 10 relates.

[65] These cannons were top caliber men, known among their peers as "top guns."

heavy in England, France, and Italy. They were decided in specialties. One of the famous universities was Bocano in Italy, which taught medicine. Bologna was in Paris for law. Oxford was another university, also in France, which helped establish Cambridge (home of the mathematical bridge). In Paris they taught arts; they had astronomy, too, which is the study of astrology and the stars.

Young men were becoming inflamed with the love of learning like Abelard.[66] Abelard was sold on logic as the solution for everything. The cream of the intellect was at the university. Schoolmasters were called pedigrees. Medieval students didn't have history because they were making it.

Theology was the one subject at universities with the most freedom to expand, explore, and express. They taught by the disputic method which was argumentive discussion between student and teacher. One German professor was fired for stabbing one too many of his colleagues in a faculty meeting. There is another case where a teacher was dismissed because he killed one too many of his students.

The universities also gave matching, multiple choice, and true and false tests. The students were the ones who steered the wagon in medieval universities, regulating prices of books and lodging and determining curriculum, fees, and the standards of teachers. Students could tell professors when to stop teaching by doing something to the hour glass.

Universities were run by guilds or corporations headed by cannons. A group of students from Bolongona formed a guild and were recognized by Emperor Frederick and granted a charter. Students were mostly from the middle medieval class; most of them were poor.

The three progressive degrees were the bachelors, masters, and doctrine. To get a master of arts degree, it took three years, which is about right. Students at the universities mastered the quadrivium—geometry, astrology, mathematics, art and music. From Euclid the Greek came geometry. The Venereal Bede, an astronomer from England, taught arithmetic.[67]

But Medieval universities still had things in common with modern ones. For one thing, the older students gave the beginners (wolves or tattle tales) a hard time. Students disciplined each other with code books passed from yellow beak upperclassmen to red beak underclassmen.

---

[66] Unfortunately Abelard also became inflamed with Heloise, but such carnal knowledge got him into deep trouble with her family.

[67] Although his title suggests that he did more with his evenings than stare at the stars.

Students even had town and gown fights like wild parties. By age 23 most of them had no teeth. The meat had to be served rotten so they could gum it. For recreation the students frequently fought. Between studying, drinking, fighting, and wenching, the yellow-beaks or younger students had a gay old time.

There were no women allowed in the universities, just a bunch of rowdy men. Violence was tolerated and people could basically do whatever they wanted because they were students. Everyone carried a sword and attended parties with lots of sex and booze. University students' wild party animal life and fertility clubs are a throwback to Medieval times.[68]

Medieval dorms or colleges were to help poor students afford city life. They could acquire food and lodging for a modest fee (that modest fee has changed since then). Also like today, they had residence halls. Lectures are still given in today's universities, but most teachers don't read. Exams are still given, but not at the end of a four- or six-year period (thank God!).

A monastery was the place for monsters.[69] Church men, or the clergy, included the nuns. These nuns were usually unmarried and from the utmost class. But the vast majority of women were neither nuns or wives.

A monastery was the place for monsters

St. Bernard was a mink who brought on some new rules. Priests preached from a pulpit that was placed on a pilpit a few feet from the ground.

Meanwhile, the pope had archbishops, bishops, abbots, cannons, and monarchs in the papal penitentiary. Once, Pope Boniface IIX went head

---

[68] These fertility clubs were the generic ancestors of today's fraternity and sorority houses, only rowdier.

[69] Just as a convent, of course, was a place for convicts.

to head with Phillip IV from France. Pope XIII made the most important declamation of social rights for the Roman Catholic Church. Many other church officials were made fiefs and vassals. Thus many were forced to carry arms.

Before Gothic architecture, Romanesque was a dark kind of gloomy place to worship, almost like a spook house. A person gets a bad image of God that way.

The idea of building a church that was less practical and earthbound was started by Abbot Sugar, a really sweet man. Sugar was a fryer that had imagination.[70] He became the emperor and leader of the Gothic times. He believed a church should be like a crown—beautiful. He wanted the church to reflect the ethereal and mystic quality of heaven.

Gothic cathedrals portrayed to the peasants that there were two powers, God and Satan, and God ran the hierarchy of the world show by being on top. So cathedrals were full of statues of Christ and other holy folk. On the top level of the tympanum, God is depicted sitting on His heavenly thorn with the saints and angles around Him. These paintings and statues were readable by the common people. They had a constant reminder of good and evil. The picture of the crucifixion from one church, for example, was made for the purpose of spreading on the story of the Bible to the illiterate mosses.

Height was a very important aspect of the Gothic age. Gothic buttresses and flying butteresses allowed for the high verticality. (A buttress is the wife of a butler.) The cathedral's pinnacles and lanterns also gave more height to the building. Gothic cathedrals had apes at the east end surrounded by the chapels.[71] The long nave was crossed perpendicularly by the transept. Also the cathedrals had beautiful stain glass windows which portrayed Biblical stories. Churches were filled with these large stain glass pictorials, especially in the celestial sections. The Christian reformers had a hay-day with their artful stain glass windows, colossus cathedrals, and holy wars.

During the Middle Ages, the thirteenth century church was a boomer. The church was at the height of its power, but it abused it through bad courts, wheeling and dealing, and some not too holy popes.

---

[70] Suger presided at collegial fish and chips parties as the fish friar while St. Bernard was the chip monk.

[71] This menagerie of low life and high life helped the illiterate pheasants, who could not understand Latin, grasp the meaning of the Sunday mass.

Cassiodorus was one good pope. St. Benedict made the central government more efficient when he was pope. Boniface VIII was a German missionary who later became pope. In Rome an Italian by the name of Urban VI was made archbishop, but since he was French, some other countries wouldn't respect him as pope.[72] Urban VI turned out to be horrible. He completely disregarded his barons' suggestions and was an overall meanie.

Ego ſum Papa.

Urban VI was an overall meanie

---

[72] Italian archbishops could become French popes only by transubstantiation.

The Roman Catholic Church, through their outspoken popes like St. Aquins (who stated that women were defective beings) and Gratian (who stated that women were not in the likeness of God) influenced a very negative attitude of women. The church did not even recognize marriage as a scared state.

During the Middle Ages they had monastic marriages, or one wife to a man. Marriage was considered sacred because of the belief that Adam and Eva got married in heaven before sin. God had made Eva out of a rib that he took from Adam. She was deformed because the rib was supposed to be bent and facing the wrong direction. This is known as the bent rib theory.

Up until the twelfth century, women were placed into three categories: aristocrats, boroughs, and peasants. Women were involved in everything; well, almost everything. They worked in breweries, coopering, gold and silver fashioning, black smithing, sales, and hotels.[73] Medieval women had the right to go to public places such as the Coliseum.[74]

Town women were mostly industrial working women who worked in different factories. The working class women were called berghers. The peasants were almost the same as slaves, but they were still free men. They were treated equally in labor and felt good about their work. Peasant women had to work out in the fields, however, and their clothes were the least nice of all the others.

Widows who chose to serve in convents were thought of as better than common women. This no-sex, less-sin approach to women reflected thoughts of the Virgin Mary.

Althea of Aquintaine set the ethical code for women of the day. Clement said that men thought illogically. Galen chimed in to say that men came from the left side of the womb. The Latin word for left is translated into dexterity, flexibility, and stability. Galen added that women came from the right side, the Latin word meaning sinister, evil, and untrustworthy. Today we see some of that anti-women view reflected by lack of a popess, a woman president, and how about Hillary Clinton?[75]

---

[73] Women ran most of the Holyday Inns, often combining their talents as brewers with those of sales and services to pilgrims, knights, and pheasant wayfarers.

[74] As the noisy blood sports in the Coliseum had ended in 409 AD, women found this arena a quiet place to meditate, far from the madding male crowd.

[75] At this date (2014), Hillary is running neither for popess nor presidentress. Being married certainly presents an impediment to attaining the former.

The church had enormous power and inflicted taxes upon the people. Often the pope sent leggets[76] (his personal ambassadors) to help the king rule. He also issued legates in which bishops were to follow strict rules and were to be superior to their dioceses.

The church and pope were good at sniffing out whatever smelled like heresy. Urban II was the pope who began the Inquestion. A court of Inquestion was established to try heretics, especially in Spain, with many torturous results. If the church didn't like one's way of life, it zapped you.

They also had certain tests to find out if a person was a witch. If they didn't bleed the presumed right way, they would be human sizzle burgers.

The Waldenses had their records burned and documents destroyed. They were just plain ol' hassled. The Paulicians taught that December 25th was not the birth of Christ, but they did teach the people about wilderness survival. Then the hermits came to the Catholic monasteries for spiritual and physical guidance.

By placing church-educated men like these in key positions, by controlling doctrines taught in universities, and by the persecution of the heretics, all this shows that the Catholic Church in fact exerted much power in Western Europe.

The thirteenth century also saw the signing of Magna Charta, which said that the king had no right to bring soldiers into a lady's house and tell her to mind them.

In Russia, the nobels were very powerful, very bull-headed, and had a hard time working together. In about 1240, Mongol hordes descended on Eastern Europe. They put off whatever contact the Ruskies had with the civilized world.

---

[76] The perambulating papal emissaries have given us the expression "to leg it" today.

7

The Bubonic Plague Struck At a Bad Time

The fourteenth century was a wild and out-of-control period. The whole thing was just one big headache.

Europe was filled with calamity, trial, and tribulation. There was a slight change in weather conditions that became known as the little ice age in Europe. Thus the century started off on a wrong foot weather-wise.

There was hardly any advancement in any particular area. People were depressed and unmotivated. Ruler after ruler failed, which then made it easier for the kings to regain power eventually. The problem of a weak government was caused mostly by having such young things in office. Also, people questioned authoritarians. Then too, many of the royal officials had not been paid in months or even years. During this calamitous century, rulers and leaders were broke and had to brick or steal to get money.[77] Soon every aspect of life was taxed. Things just weren't working out and no one seemed to try to fix it. With no sleep or food, France had a chance to win back their land and send England back to their own land. The Jews finally extinguished the flu by burning London down. Then the Bergourias also revolted, but their self-governments collapsed as well.

Economically, the western world was a mess as usual. Trade was low because at the time, new and better ideas weren't being manufactured.

Everything had reached its limit. No food was being produced because there was no empty, fertile lands and no goods were being

---

[77] Hence the expression "gold-bricking," or passing off inferior bars of metal as genuine gold to recoup their unpaid salaries.

manufactured. Therefore, trade was stopped. Because the people did not have the money, the government could not get blood from a stone.[78] Poverty was real now, not something pursued by those trying to be holy.

The fourteenth century saw the outburst of plagues—bubonic, spellnic, pneumonic, sepathimic and nobonic. The bubonic plague was mainly caused by bad hygiene, from the uncleanliness of poverty, and was mostly transported by animals and bugs such as black rats, fleas, and flies. It was also associated with glaciers and the ice age.

The plague, known as the Black Death, struck at a bad time. This plague was the cream on the cake, for it pushed the people over the edge and made them emotionally unstable, which coupled with economic depression and troubles with the church, topped the cake. People started going crazy. They would get beat with whips and chains and sticks. By this time their form of dress was ostentatious and bizarre.

The plague came to Europe in 1331 via Mongolia. It entered through the Black Sea ports of Italy from the traders of Asia, riding on the backs of black rats who came to Europe on board the Mongol ships when the Mongols decided to expand to other territories. The plague spread through Spain, France, and then it hit Europe with a big bang. Then it struck almost one-third of the population of the Middle East. Finally, it was spread across Asia by the Mongons.

It was carried on rats' fleas and they bit women and children. The plague attacked the limbic system of the body through the lymph noids.[79] People's undernourished condition lowered their bodies' strength and resistance, inviting the nasty bacterium, called Yersinia Pestis, to invade. This was thought of as the bleu-bonic plague. One of the symptoms was uncontrollable sneezing. If you got that, you were in for it.

This disease, which was contagious through touch, tore gaps and holes in cities and towns. It killed many peasants and thus made them more valuable. So they demanded less cents and more wages. Peasants and surfs were able to leave the farms and start skilled craft industries after the Bubonic Plague passed through.

The Black Death caused 200,000,000 deaths. It whipped out 25%-50% of Europe's population, resulting in the worst disaster ever recorded. This disaster killed almost all the people, including animals.

---

[78] Swords were being pulled from stones in those days but lack of money cramped magicians' attempts to squeeze blood from stones.

[79] Prior to the Scientific Revolution, human bodies had limbic systems and noids, but since the sixteenth century, these systems have atrophied as a result of the paradigm shift.

The massive loss of life was trying on the soles. There was a 10% decline in population. This overpopulation led to famine. People were terrified of this terrible disease; even survivors came to think of life as being cheap and worthless. Because of the plague, people had mass alcohol and sex orgies. An uproar of anti-semitis followed the plague. They believed that the Jews were spreading it by pouring poison into the village wells.

The Jews, however, were not affected by the plague or rioting because they had cleaner living habits. They didn't live in Europe where it was filthy. The disease was spread a lot by priests going from house to house giving people their last writes.[80]

All in all, the bubonic plague was a very indignant way to die. But then, death was a problem at this time even more so than ever.

Death was a problem at this time
even more so than ever

The people who did die, they would bury under the statues which meant a great deal to them in the time they lived. The Black Plague was

---

[80] This "last writes" theory, implying the possibility of plague-ridden pens and infected ink, deserves further investigation.

also one of the reasons the European economy was going down the tubes.

The ring around the rose song represented the rosary beads that people used to pray for others so they wouldn't get sick during the plague. Bassaccio wrote about ten pilgrims fleeing the effects of this Black Death, seeking beauty and liberation.

The Peasant Rebellion in 1831 happened because the peasants were being trodden upon.[81] The peasants of Europe were tired of the high price of wages, given the low standards of living and increasing amount of taxes.

The fourteenth century was the century where Europe tried to put themselves back together, and while doing this, they found out about themselves. This caused many people to wonder what next, and whenever people think like that, they go and get what they want.

This is one of the reasons for the peasant revolt. The peasants just got tired of being peasants. They were in the majority now; kings no longer held high rank. The peasant rivalry occurred because the monasteries were raising revenues by placing tax poles on all adults in the population. The peasants' rising expectations also caused the uprising, which was led by preacher John Bell and peasant Wyat Tylor.

The peasants marched on London and tried to get Richard III to eliminate the poll tax. He promised he would, but instead, he didn't, so the peasants killed him and got the tax eliminated (King Richard is also said to have been murdered by some historians; his real fate is uncertain). The peasants then destroyed many buildings and records and land, but were mercilessly put down. It was quite successful, however, until Wyat Tylor was killed, then it failed. In France, the peasants revolted in 1357 in the Jaquist Revolt.

During the fourteenth century, the tripartite system of clergy, nobility, and laborers fell apart. Landlords were now forced to live by the lower standards of society. Their wages were lowered because the prices of help went up.

The Babylonian Captivity was also in action during the fourteenth century, while the Great Schism was also in full swing. The pope was not in Rome, however, when the church was captured by the Babylonians.

King Philip IV had tried to imprison a French bishop, which was illegal without papal permission, and Boniface threatened to extradite Philip from the church. This angered Philip, who attacked the pope and

---

[81] That a fourteenth century peasant revolt could occur in 1831 demonstrates the time warp theory, which, like continental drift, happened more frequently in those days than it does today.

captured him. Even though the pope was let go, he could not take what was happening very well and died a month later.

Rome, not wanting the papal power to diminish, quickly gathered together the cardinals and elected an archbishop, Urgent VI. After his death, the cardinals elected another pope by the name of Utopia IV who turned against them, so they denounced him and elected another pope. Both popes were claiming authority from God and both said the other was the anti-Christ. The popes were very much under the control of the church. Much of the time, the empire and the church collaborated on similar interests. Churchmen called conciliarists included Ocknard from England, Jean Gersen from France, and Mussolini from Italy.[82]

Following the Babylonian Captivity, the Great Schism was from 1378 to 1412. It was a war between Christians and Jews. Clement V was forced into subservience to the papacy in Avignon. The pope made bills, was charged with heresy, and moved again to Asantine. This move and abuse created stress, turmoil, problems and commoners' unhappiness with the papacy.

There was a dual papacy for about 40 years known as the Great Schift. The schift began when Avignon died and the Roman people decided they didn't want to lose money to the papacy anymore. During this time, rulers like Henry IV and Frederic Barbarosa tried to set up anti-popes. All of these elections and anti-popes bewildered the people of Europe. They were thinking, Will the real pope please stand up? So the papacy moved back to Rome, Italy, under George XI.[83]

Over in England, John Wycliffe was called the "Morning Star of the Reformation" because he came out of the obscurity and chaos of the Dark Ages. Just as the morning star gives hope to the arriving dawn about 3 a.m., Wycliffe laid a deep and steadfast hope for the dawn of the Reformation. He studied at Balliol College, Oxford, and took government, socialism, history, cannon law, theology, secular law, and both the trivium and the octavium.[84] He became quite versed in cannon law.

Wycliffe believed that the Bible was the infallow law of God. His Bible teachings inspired Martin Luther, and through him the Seventh-

---

[82] That the Ancient Babylonians could invade Medieval Rome while the future dictator Mussolini was writing treatises on conciliarism demonstrates the potency of the time warp phenomenon in those days.

[83] This little-known English pope (like his ten predecessors) is often omitted from the traditional lists of the bishops of Rome.

[84] Balliol College established a famous foundary for casting the new cannon and had a book bindery to publish the octavo editions of John Bell and Wyat Tylor's socialist manuscripts.

day Adventist Church was started. He felt that no prayers or candles should be given to the dead; they are dead, so don't bother them. This is called disendowment and means that since the dead are at rest, people need not pray or pay for their soles.[85] Wycliffe also preached civil domino—that the church should give up its properties to the state as well as tax money.

The Catholic Church also took away individual Bibles from each individual, and Wycliffe said they should give them back. He also struck out against the monastic friars.[86] Wycliffe became the chaplin of the king of England and was protected by King Edward III of Austrasia as well as by John of Gaul. His followers were called Howards, Lombards, or Lollards, and were widely persecuted. They were punished by the king for spreading the truth.

Wycliffe played important roles such as writing the Vulgate Bible in English with the help of Martin Luther of Germany, Hus and Jerome, Herdman and Purvey of England.[87] The followers of John Hus were called Hussians. One of Wycliffe's goals was for every farmer and plowboy to have a Bible, but the printing press came into existence almost 70 years later.

The pope was a fairly good person, but Wycliffe had his doubts about him. One day Wycliffe found out that the pope was gone and when he tracked him down, he begged him to come back to the original ways and back to the truth. During the rain of Henry V, three papal bulls from the universities, kings, and parliament were hurled against Wycliffe by Urban III. This did not stop him, for he refused to be cowed by these bulls. Instead, he cowed them all. Gregory XI hated Wycliffe so much that he sent three more papal bowls of excommunication against him.

When it looked like Wycliffe was on his death bed, the fryers came to him and asked him to repent. He told them he would keep preaching the truth and got up out of bed. The fryers fled in fear. Wycliffe was paralyzed at the age of 56 and died of a stork in 1584, after which he was burned at the stake in 1384.[88]

---

[85] And quite logically so, for after burial, the dead are not likely to do much walking or need new shoes.

[86] This occurred in the third inning, as Wycliffe's Chip Monks played the Fish Friars on July 22, 1374.

[87] The time warp phenomenon extended northward from Italy into England, enabling the sixteenth-century Luther and the fifteenth-century Hus and Jerome to assist the fourteenth-century Wycliffe in this task.

[88] Although death by storks was common in those days, dying twice at 200-year intervals was not, and this time warp phenomenon gave Wycliffe some distinction.

Wycliffe died of a stork

Over in France, the French refused to put Edward III on the French thrown and elected their own King Louis IX who didn't have all his senses functioning. The Hundred Years' War lasted from May 1337 to October 1473 under Edward III. It was about the only thing he and his barons could agree on. It was another fourteenth century tragedy, interspersed with short peaces. There's no good reason why it had to last as long as it did, but nevertheless, it did.

Edward III was hungrier and hungrier for more and more wealth and land. Gregory the Great was another king who fought in the Hundred Years' War, but his subjects knew they had the right to partition the king.

First there was the Hundred Years' War, Part One; then later, there was the Hundred Years' War, Part Two.[89] The Hundred Years' Wars weren't beneficial because the people tended to scrabble back home while the king and generals were off fighting. France and England were the warring nations and the peasants were the pawns. During the years of

[89] This wildly popular war was later made into a mini-series called "The Winds of War."

truce, the unemployed soldiers gorged up and romped around the French country side stealing and killing. The English bow could shoot six arrows at a time, so up until 1915 at Agincourt the English seemed to be conquering.

During the Black Prince's campaigns, Edward, the Prince of Whales, burned villages and unfortified towns, ravaged the lands and stole everything that had value. Then the French started defeating the English with their longbows. The Port of Flanders was loyal to England and gave the French a heck of a time. The French knights' charge was useless against the cannon.

Then Joan of Arch joined the scene. Much of the victory for France was due to the leadership of Joan, a very good Christian who suffered a lot. She had a mission and said, Nothing doing, to the English. She convinced the Dauphin, Charles VII, to take the thrown.[90] Finally, the French burned her at the steak for her part in the French invasion.

This rallied the English, who won the war, and in the end, only Callet was in the hands of the French. Joan's treatment shows that misogamy, the hatred of women, stemmed from mythical beliefs that women were witches. Most witches were women over 50 years of age, maidservants, pheasants, single or widowed. But by the end of the Middle Ages, there was a change in attitude. Women were now respected because of the fact that they were able to give birth.

Thus the many events of the fourteenth century, such as the Black Death, the church losing power, war, natural disasters, all led to an unpleasant era to be alive in, much less dead in.

---

[90] The frequency with which kings were overthrown in those days explains the quaint spelling of "throne" found in Medieval manuscripts.

8

The Renaissance Was an Enthusiasm For Classical Iniquity

The Renaissance was probably a great time in history. The term Renaissance means "maturity, growing up," because the Renaissance came right after the experiences of the calamitous fourteenth century. People had learned from past experiences and had new ideas about their purpose in life. The church had undergone division, but was now united. Popes such as Julius VI showed religious themes during the Renaissance. People were capable of creating great works of art. The thought of the times was fresh and new, almost like a spring after winter. Themes of Individualism, Humanism, and Secularism all whispered of man's involvement with man, for this was the age when man's measure mattered the most.

The seven great powers of Europe at this time were gravity, electricity, steam, gas, flywheels, motors, and Mr. Floyd George. Italy had five major city-states: Milan, Florence, Papal States, Venice, and Nobles. Condortinnis were leaders of mercenary troops for these city-states and came around whenever an energy crisis arose.

The Renaissance put a new direction to thought and art. Da Vince was more than an artist; he was a scientist. Nature was his text book; his works and sketches were his exams. He removed the myth affixed to man and God and separated them once and for all. Raphael showed in one of his paintings a school with Plato and some other wise guy from Ancient Greece.

All the women of this period must have been overweight because they were all portrayed that way in the paintings. It was fashionable— maybe because the men wanted something big to hug.

In courtly love tradition, if two people discussed something, it was later said to be love. Castiglione's book, *The Art of Courtly Love*, told men how to get the women that caught their eye. In 1431 the first women's libber spoke up—Christine Pezer—and after her, Cathrine Zell spoke up for women's rights. Whether a seamstress or a cook or maybe a smith or a copper, women were laborers and were considered workers the same as males. But women still remained on the back burner, although a few areas in religion, social gatherings, and antislavery groups were contributed to by women. Still, they didn't really benefit from the Renaissance.

One Renaissance area in which new discoveries were made was architecture, as when Fillipo Bruneshelski sought ways to raise a dome on the cathedral he was building in Florence.[91] He found himself very interesting and he believed that anyone who had done excellence should write a story of themselves.

Education in literachure, grammer, and philosy was the primary concept of humanism. Humanism is an enthusiasm for classical iniquity. This growing secularism was best seen in Florence, the hotbed of the Renaissance.[92] Secularism involved all the worry about balance of much and little, model pads, new threads, corner delis, wine, women, and song. The Renaissance was an explosion of man's intellectual mind in the arts.

An enthusiasm for classical iniquity

---

[91] This Italo-Polish connection in Renaissance architecture deserves further study by scholars.

[92] While many Humanists, among them Boccaccio, warmed with appreciation for classical iniquity, the friar Savonarola made things hot in Florence for those who possessed iniquitous objects.

9

Martin Luther Was a Son of a Pheasant Miner

The morals of the Medieval church sank as immorality hit. Hus and Scolorati both tried reforming the Catholic Church, but both were fried as human vegeburgers by the church that believed in "thou shalt burn thy neighbor."

The problem of pluralism was one where there was an overabundance of these right monks living the high life. There was a saint for every illness or pain. As for relics, they would see the baby skull of one saint, go to a different city and see the adult leg of the same saint. As for simony, priests could get money by selling okays for sin.

One of the problems in the Catholic church was absenteeism, which was the failure to appear. Another problem that led to the Reformation was the attitude of immortality that the Catholic monks, priests, and deacons had (a deacon is the lowest kind of Christian).

The people, popes, rulers—all became more secular in their thinking. Even the pope had sculptures of something done of his illegitimate sons scattered about the Vaccuum, a large empty space where the popes live in Rome.

The popes were a horrid moral example as they fought among one another for leadership: divine beings acting in an earthly way. Popes were trying to squeeze blood out of a turnip.[93] Sextus IV was probably the forefather of the "Price is Right" game show because of his idea that he,

---

[93] This activity proved only slightly more successful than the Medieval attempt to squeeze blood from rocks.

through his doctrine, was powerful enough to save from purgatory or devastation if the price was right.

Indulgences were being sold furiously, even by street corner vendors like Tetzel. Johann Tetzel, like the monk Sugar, helped translate the Bible into the German Binocular Version.[94]

Priests could get money by selling okays for sin

Tetzel was also a famous poet who wrote poems about indulgences and sold them in front of the castle church at Wittenberg. An indulgence was a document that showed that one had paid for one's penance or sins. The people also began to pay money to keep their relatives in purgatory longer or to try to get them into heaven. Tetzel's sales jingle was, "As soon as the coin clings, the soul begins to spring." He traveled about

---

[94] The Binocular Version was a special large-print edition for the visually impaired.

obtaining money which was supposed to go to the building of Saint Peter's Cathedral in Rome, but most of the ill-gotten lute ended up in the pockets of the Count of Mainze.[95]

About this time a frier and professor of Bible in the University of Wintenberg began objecting to teachings like there is a ladder going to heaven, or every person who is dead can be prayed and gotten out of purgery. Some thought that by confessing (and paying the priest for confession), it would earn them points. Funds from the sale of these indulgences were being put into a Fluger bank. Soon the Reformation was on because people started not wanting to pay for a free ticket to the Kingdom. Thus anyone of true will and drive to know the truth and make it to heaven would not want to go via the Catholic Church Express.

Up rose Martin Luther, a son of a pheasant gone to a miner's father.[96] Luther flageleted himself; he whipped himself so much that he passed out. He gave the Holy Roman Empire the extra push it needed to start the reformation ball rolling.

Luther thought indulgences were malarchy. So on October 31, 1517, he posted his 95 theses on the door of the Castle Church in Woodward. In his theses, he attacked indulgences and defied Tetzel who taught that penances actually took dead relatives out of hell. Surely Tetzel would have starved if the only people around had been like Luther.

Then in 1651, Luther nailed 95 more theses to the church door at Wittenburg, followed in 1917 by the nailing of 99 theses on the church doors in Vicksburg.[97] His theses ended up in the hands of the archbishop of money and Fugger banking.

Being a brilliant theologician, Luther disagreed with many of the church's ways. He had realized after many years in the monkery that the truth was righteousness by faith.[98] He founded Lutheranism, which was a part of Normandy. He also believed that the monasteries were a bad way of life, so he went so far as to marry a nun, having six kids and living happily ever after.

He believed that God wanted everyone to witness and that one didn't need to be celibate to witness. He didn't believe in prayers for the dead,

---

[95] According to Peter Schickele, the count was quite musically inclined and played several instruments, the lute among them.

[96] Of all the charges leveled against Luther by his enemies, that of buggery is certainly the most vile.

[97] The 95 Theses enjoyed widespread popularity on at least two continents. For Southern Baptists, four new ones were added in 1917.

[98] This primate truth dawned clearly on Luther's mind following several years as a zoo keeper in Frankfurt-am-Main.

since they were dead prayers and nothing else could help their eternal destiny. Instead, he taught the priesthood of believers and that the Bible is the soul truth. Finally, at the Diet of Worms, the council told him to shape up or ship out—he chose to ship out.

The Catholic church believed strongly in family and marriage. They strongly taught abstinence in sex. They preferred holiness over sex. Because it was so hard for men to stay chaste, they were forced to be married once their chains of lust were broken. To make marriage purposeful, the procreation of children was encouraged. Luther saw marriage as an excuse to cover up (or a way of avoiding) the sin of sex.

So during this time there was a new look at mutual love between man and wife. Men and women were treated symmetrically during the Protestant Reformation. Some women managed to stay out of nunnery clothes so that they could do their work in the community. But because of the elimination of monasticism, women were left with few career alternatives.

John Calvin, a Frenchman residing in Geneva in 1536, wrote *Institutes of Christian Religion* and entitled it TULIP.[99] It was a handbook of Protestantism. Calvin studied many of the writings of Gwingli. He believed that God chose only a few people whom he graced.

Calvin was not particularly known for flowery orations, but his teachings did blossom during and after the Reformation. Calvinists taught a simpler, easy-going, fulfilled art. Thus, people like John Calvin and Martin Luther King led out in the Reformation, even though this was a dangerous act.

The Simons were led by a man named Mennon from which are derived the name Mennonites.[100] But most of these reformers were either burned at the steak, tourchered to death, or shortened by a head, which directly hindered their work.

The Tudor family was greatly involved in the politics of England. The pope was under the influence of Charles V who was the nephew of Anne Boylen, the hydra who was married to Henry VIII. When he cut her head off, another sprung up. Eventually, he had six wives. Maybe he just didn't have enough excitement in his life.

---

[99] This clever ploy enabled Calvin to evade censorship in France since the police thought his treatise was a harmless gardening journal.

[100] Because Mennon enjoyed a lucrative income from the after-shave business, his movement had a well-financed evangelistic outreach.

Archbishop Cranmer of Canterbury opposed Catholicism on Ireland. He built up anticlerical sentiment and forced the English clergy to recognize the pope as the Supreme Head of the Church of England. Archbishop Wolsey saved his life by dying on the way from York to London. Then the nobels and peasants rebelled in the English Rose War because the open field system was advantageous to the common, small farmers and collergerates.

After King Edward VI came Mary Tutor, who was hated because she married Philip II of Scotland, which went against all tradition. Mary burned 282 persons at the steak. Most tried to flee to places such as Germany and Switzerland; among them was John Hus.[101] Other Protestant leaders, like John Locke, escaped to Scotland. John Knox then established Presbyterianism in Sweden, where liberty of conscience meant doing wrong and not worrying about it afterward.

When England was placed under an interdict, the pope stopped all births, marriages, and deaths for a year.[102] In 1570, after the pope was excommunicated, Elizabeth I was forced to deal with the overzealous Catholics who denied her right to rule as traitors. The Catholics tried to replace her with Mary Stuart, otherwise known as Bloody Mary of Scots. But Mary married the French King Frederick II.

Elizabeth was tall and thin, but she was a stout Protestant. She was, in fact, the longest queen to rule back then.

The Protestant zealots wanted Mary of Scots, a very French and a very Protestant person, to succeed Elizabeth. Protestant extremists called themselves Puritans because they wanted to purify the church of its doings. But Elizabeth hooked up with Cecil and built a strong kingdom.

Unlike her mother, Ann Boleyn, Elizabeth I did not marry Phillip II from Spain.[103] "Those melodious bursts that fill the spacious days of great Elizabeth" referred to the songs the Queen used to write in her spare time.

Queen Elizabeth rode a white horse from Kenilworth through Coventry with nothing on, and Raleigh offered her his cloak. One day after there

---

[101] Having been burned at the stake once already in the fifteenth century, Hus had no desire to be fried again in the sixteenth century, so he fled, allegedly to Germany to live among his beloved Hussians.

[102] How Clement VII accomplished this remains a tightly guarded secret at the Vatican even today.

[103] Elizabeth would have lost her title of "The Virgin Queen" had she married Europe's most eligible bachelor. This would have required drastic changes in poems written in her honor and would have left the state of Virginia undiscovered.

had been a lot of rain, he threw his cloak in a puddle and the Queen stepped dryly over. Lord Raleigh was also the first to see the Invisible Armada. He was also once put out when his servant found him with fire in his head, smoking.

Philip abhorred heresy and unbelief with a holy hatred and said that he would rather be king of a desert than to live in a land of heretics. Spain decided they had better step in to English affairs. They thought the Protestants were getting a little carried away in the Netherlands, so they marched in with the Duke of Alba in command.

Queen Elizabeth was tall and thin, but she was a stout Protestant

Huguenots were French Protestants, usually Catholic.[104] Catherine de Medici convinced her son in the Battle of St. Patrick to slay these Huguenots, especially after King Francis I was captured by the Huguenots. This act gave the Catholics a motive to persecute Protestants.

---

[104] Seldom has Catholicism been so truly universal as during this era.

Witchcraft was also becoming a big thing now. About 80% of women were considered witches in the sixteenth century. Some witches were said to practice cantabalism.[105]

Witchcraft was also becoming a big thing now

---

[105] The Inquisition considered the eating of both humans (cannibalism) and cantaloupes (cantabalism) as highly immoral acts. Later, eating red tomatoes (vegetarianism) was added to the list of verboten foods.

10

In 1522 the Cape of Good Hope Set Sail

The general unrest of the sixteenth century was evident at a point of restlessness. Europe was ready for an Age of Discovery because Europeans longed for the old stability of the past. They also began to get restless for something new, something to add zest to their lives. Thus, it was no wonder that they turned to the mysterious seas with their longings, consequently ushering in the Age of Discovery. Europeans also had an itch and were bored so they wanted to take an adventure.[106]

Spain had few people and the Dutch had many in their army, but the Spanish had the help of the Queen's Spanish Armada. The Spanish were given papal bulls to convert and nurture the heathen people in the Christian faith. They took it very seriously.[107] The people who came to America found Indians, but no people.

Europeans also used spices to cure their meat, make deodorant, and mix up their Old Spice after shave. Spices were spread on the body to help cover body stench until next month's bath. Many times in the winter, people would sew their clothes on and not take them off until spring.[108]

---

[106] Such persistent itching was a legacy of the Bubonic Plague which some families inherited through their limbic systems. It gradually disappeared when bathing became popular in the seventeenth century.

[107] That is, the Spanish took it very seriously; the bulls and the natives took Christianity somewhat less seriously.

[108] This gave rise to the popular phrases, "It's all sewed up!" and "A stitch in time saves nine," meaning nine more months of not having to change clothes.

The legend of Prester John led John II of Portugal to search for the old faithful apostal in places like Ababab in Ethiopia, where John was a prester.

At this time, the people were more prepared technologically and sycologically for long voyages on the sea. The ships were improved. The Portuguese constructed a new ship, the *squat*, which was a three-masted one, able to sail the seas to the wind. They also designed a two-masted latin-rig. Bartolome de las Casas invented the first set of water wings.[109]

Also, navigational tools were developed, such as the astrolabe, which gave the sailors latitude positions; the compass, which gave them direction at night; and the Portugal charts which enabled sailors to identify ports. Portolan charts were maps that gave sailors better assurance of what harbor, bay, and land mass they were near. Sailors who were first in an area would draw these and then pass them on to other sailors going in that direction.[110] Ships also used the German and Italian city-states as a guide. These were replaced by monarchies which were much easier to spot from the sea.[111]

Discoveries in other worlds made Europeans realize that they were not the only humans around. When they landed in the Americas, they had to face the Indians. Sometimes the Indians would attack. Sometimes the explorers would attack. But the men had a good time shedding blood.[112] They could also find Indian women to enjoy their leisure time with. Because the Indians used as cheap labor weren't paid well, they weren't fed, and they were very susceptible to European diseases such as smallpox and typho. On the low coastal plains of Mexico, for example, yellow fever was very popular.

Some of the West Indies Islands were subject to hurricanes and torpedoes. There was always something happening on these explorations!

Franciscan friers and the Polos of Venice discovered the steps, a land route to China. Lief Ericson was a Spanish expeditioner and a famous rock star, while Ceasare Borgia was just a man of that era.

---

[109] Water-winged ships confused the sea monsters into thinking the squat was another sea creature; hence more explorers on squats got through uneaten than those who sailed on caravels, galleons, or naos.

[110] Maps could be sent via the highly sophisticated navel internet, also invented at this time.

[111] The rise of Divine Light Monarchies is a major phenomenon of this era, as chapter 14 explains.

[112] It was much more civilized shedding one another's blood than trying to extract blood from rocks and turnips as their ancestors had done.

*The West Indies Islands were subject
to hurricanes and torpedoes*

In 1522 the Cape of Good Hope set sail around the world.[113] Vasco de Gama rounded the cape and sailed to the Colient. Vasco was a Renaissance explorer who discovered Portugal, then became a French explorer who helped in the Portuguese exploration. He was the first to sail around India. In Portugal, Dias in 1488 discovered the southern tip of Spain. Ferdinand Magellan also sailed for Portugal, but first he married Isabella so their son Henry would be the king of Spain.[114] Prince Henry married seven times in order to have a son to share his throne.

---

[113] The frequency of continental drifting in those days explains why it took the Portuguese so long to find the cape and sail around it in 1486.

[114] Long before Fulbright Fellowships, Magellan and the Queen created Isabella Fellowships to fund global exploration.

Magellan was the first to sail around South America (now called the Magellan Straights) and around the world (although he met his death by the natives of the Philippians). Cortes conquered the Aztecs by force with just a few hundred men, horses, and a few canons. In Mexico, zambos (another name for zombies) were persons who stayed up all night studying. Misquitos were children born to black and white parents.

Christopher Columbus was a Beloise sailor. He landed on Little Spain. Balboa discovered the Pacific Ocean and sailed around the globe. Girolamo Savonarola was also a Spanish explorer. Francis Drake was an Italian explorer.

The Scientific Revolution made great contributions, like mathematical explanations of the universe, hermit magic, and new available books. Scientists of the day held the view of the geocentric model of the universe with the earth at the center, surrounded by the sun, the moon, the planets, the stars, then the angles and finally God. In the Middle Ages, astronomy had been very midevil in thought. They thought the earth was elliptical and imperfect, and that God was in heaven or somewhere in the moons.

Many contributions were made in astronomy by Kepler, Kephart, Brahe, Galleo and others. Galleo used a teleosocope for the first time. He got it from a lense grinder in Ireland. Kibbel still believed that the moon orbited around the planets. Tye Breye was known for using the spyglass; he also made improvements in it. He also wrote a book called the *Starry Messenger*. Ptolemy built the castle in England with a library and observatory where he did most of his studying. The compass, invented by Leevenhoek, the microscope, the ascrolade, and advances in printing methods and art all helped in the other fields.

11

Charles I Was a
Not-So-Good Dude

The problem in England was that every other king was Catholic and every other king was Protestant. Of these, Charles I was a not-so-good dude.

The Long Parliament forced Charles to sign a Petition of Rights of which there were two parts. One—no taxation without Parliamentary consent, and two—it just slipped my mind.[115] So Charles said, The heck with Parliament, and ruled without it for the next eleven years. He took the title Lord Protector instead of king. He tried writing a written constitution, but after awhile, realized that the people weren't ready for this religious toleration. Then came the beheading of Charles I: he was the first of any nobel to win such a prize!

Oliver Cromwell was an Englishman, the right hand man of Louis VIII. He became an English poet who wrote literature for Queen Elizabeth, who had to marry Philip II, who was a Catholic, so there was division right in the home.

The Rump Parliament consisted entirely of Cromwell's stalactites. During his rule, there was quite a bit of religious toleration. He was a reformer who was finally burned at the stake.

The English Navigation Acts hurt the Dutch bad and soon navel wars broke out between the Dutch and English. The Dutch War gave France Falanders.

---

[115] The Petition of Rights, among other important parliamentary documents, always seemed to slip Charles I's mind also. This led to major problems, as on January 30, 1649 when he simply lost his head.

Charles II, son of Louis, mounted his thrown with the idea of regaining absolutist monarchy for a governing mode. He never stamped his foot down on the trend towards Constitutional Monarchy, however. Under his reign, Margaret Fell, a Quacker, organized a Women's Petition in 1659.

Charles had signed an agreement with King Louis VXI of France in 1670 stating in part that he would become a Catholic and make England a Catholic commonwealth when the opportunity arose, which it never did. He passed the Test Act in 1673, which declared only the Angelicans could hold military or civil offices. The Cavalier Parliament convened from 1661 to 1679. They in essence ruled the king because they held his financial pockets. Then came the Great Plague of 1665 and the Great Fire of 1666 which in London certainly depressed many a poor soul.[116]

Charles was the first of any nobel to win such a prize

James II came into power. He was the grandson of Louis XIV. Eventually, after James II's continued attempts to rule absolute, even his supporters, the Wigs in Parliament, got tired of him, turned against him, and invited William the Orange to come and become king of England.[117] The Glorious Revolution came soon after James II had taken the thrown.

---

[116] According to Pepys' diary, the fire was equally hard on people's soles.

[117] William the Orange, a real fruitcake in many respects, was the great-grandfather of Robert Peel.

Defeated, James flew to France with the support of Louis XIV,[118] taking his young son with him. This young pretender, known as James II, was so called because it was pretended that he was born in a frying pan.

During this time, England was truly putting its power on the Cabinet and Parliament, dispersing it, while France was focusing or concentrating it. In effect, the Glorious Revolution of 1866 limited the power of the monarchy. The Habea Corpus Act was passed, stating that no one need stay in prison longer than he liked. Finally, the religious quails were put to an end by the Toleration Act.

The Wigs in Parliament

---

[118] KLM Airlines provided James a royal first-class seat from London to Paris.

12

Somehow France Survived Until Richelieu Arrived

Henry IV was a well-liked, tolerant king nicknamed the "Val Galant," meaning a gay old spark because he liked to make out with the young girls. Unfortunately, the works of Henry IV and of his minister Sullen went into ruins. Sullen hired farmers to collect the taxes.

Henry IV was the first French monarch to bring peace, order, and prosperity to France. Before him, France lived in a time of incredible term oil, full of luting and destruction, and the citizens were looking for something to follow. Henry enforced the peace by traveling from providence to providence and overseeing the town governmental elections. This started giving the monarchy more power. He avoided war with other countries by maintaining peace with them.[119] The Thirty Years' War, which lasted from 1648 to 1698, finally ceased after the sixteenth century when Henry IV began his reign from 1589 to 1610.

Unfortunately, King Henry was assassinated by a fanatical Catholic in 1610 and his wife Marie de Medicinis was regent. She solved problems by bribing people with money, titles, or privileges. This made certain people very greedy and made the queen a pushover. After a little while, Queen de Medicinis switched sides to the Protestant side in France when the Duke of Guise (who was Catholic) grew very powerful. Catherine de Medicinis was well aware of the rising power of the Huguenots (who were nicknamed the Roundheads because they typically shaved their heads). These Huguenots were the Protestants of the shopkeepers, pheasants, and even the nobility.

---

[119] Henry IV pioneered this method of avoiding war; none better has ever been found since his era.

A time of incredible term oil, full of luting and destruction

After Sullen and Henry IV, the estates-general was summoned by Anne of Australia to meet. Somehow France survived until Richelieu arrived. Richelieu was a tough guy who got things accomplished. A very shrew man, but very well liked, he was also a Huguenot. He had four main objectives he wanted to achieve: (1) to be rid of the Huguenots, (2) to put nobles in their rightful place, (3) to stop the Hapsburgs from interfering in France's control, and (4) to destroy the power of the Ostrogoths.[120] His political creed was *Rotate d'etat*. He sought to develop the power and prestige of the monarchy and to bring down the nobles' power.

---

[120] At this point, it is helpful to recall the time warp phenomenon.

To create order and stop all the fighting, Richelieu outlawed fights and duels, punished by death. This took a bite out of crime. He put up *raison de atet*—good of the state was supreme.

Richelieu had many spies that were looking out for him. He wanted to zap the nobles, so he developed a net of spies on the nobles and in the end he had weakened their power and could replace some of them in offices by the so-called instants. Then he attacked the Hasburgs, but this war he did not finish before his death. When both Louis and the Cardinal Richelieu died, the soon-to-be-great Louis IVX took reign, but being too young, Mazarin was placed in command.

With the hatred of high taxes, a group known as the Fronde (a game played in which slots are thrown at passing carriages) began to rebel. But the Fronde, who were judges in the Parlement, were not very happy with Mazarin's ideas. Mazarin and DeFronte came into power in 1643. Then Matzaline wanted the absolute form of government, so he began a set of wars known as the forde that made him extremely unpopular and he was eventually run out of the country.

After the rebellion fizzled out, Mazarin continued the war with Spain, called La Gloira, until France was victorious. Then he was appointed commander of the Spanish Armada. In 1661 Mazarin died, leaving many government problems behind. So Louis VIX declared that there would be absolute monarchy and he would be his own prime minister.

Meanwhile, the French army was growing, more ships were being built, and more mercenaries were being paid to serve on the front line. Victories like that in 1668 against the Australians for the deliverance of the Australian throne were all for the glory of the king.

Soon the French were either all Catholic or dead—those with any sanity chose Catholic. Huguenots were still being persecuted for their faith and were still demanding religious intolerance.[121] So in 1685, the Huguenots had to convert, either become Protestant, leave the country, or work on the galleys.

Over in Germany, the Catholics and the Lutherans had not fought each other from the time of the Peace of Augusberger in 1555. But then the greatest blow of all fell because of the Thirty Years' War from 1618 to 1678.[122] The war brought many who just wanted to control things. These big shots of the war would take control of the little states, controlling tariffs, trading, and also making it more difficult to travel. This stirred up

---

[121] Which the Catholics, to their credit, were eager to grant them.

[122] The Thirty Years' War came in two parts: Part I (1618-1648) and Part II (1648-1678). Things went so well during the first part that several nations demanded an encore.

the German Catholic princes, especially Maximilian of Bolivia, to form the Catholic League in retaliation to the Protestant Union in 1609. Germany was the center for trade in Europe, but during the Thirty Years' War, it stomped it.

In Bohemia, the Protestants were furious, so they literally threw the regents out the window; luckily they landed in a manure pile that saved their lives. The war, however, killed one-third of the population of Bohemia and England.

In the Swedish-French period of the war under Richelieu of the Swedes, Louis XIII of France entered the war openly with the Protestants and ruthlessly marched through Germany killing one-third of the population. Then came Scotland with Gustavus Adolphus as its leader. Meanwhile, Gustavus Agustus, the Swedish king, took up the protest banner next. Then the Dutch were quickly defeated by a professional soldier, Wallenstein, who had offered his services to the Empire.

No one knows why Wallenstein got involved, but he did a wonderful job of cracking the Protestant resistance. However, Ferdinand recognized this skill and saw him as a threat. Therefore, he had him assassinated, which was a dirty trick.

Those with any sanity chose Catholic

13

Louis XIV Usually Showered Every Other Week

On a hunting trip, Louis XIII and Ann of Arbor were finally put together and their differences were solved. Louis XIV was born. Louis XIV was the one powerful influence in France from 1575 to 1715. Though it is noteworthy that Louis reigned for so long, his whole high-styled life didn't appeal to some people in the least.

Louis called himself *Le Roi Moi*. He wanted everyone to look up to him, so he took the emblem *Le Foi Lesilil*. His personal absolutism was also reflected in his using the phrase *"raisin de tate."*[123] He was fond of saying *"Le Roi Soleil"* or "I Rule Alone." The rising of the king, when Louis awoke, was almost like a party guest for ceremony. The nobles were required to be at Louis XIV's awakening and help him dress, and when he went to sleep, to tuck him in.

Louis believed he was the state. He had the power to make or break rules (he ended up doing the ruling for the country in only four visits to the committees). The king, along with the help of his minister Bussuety, believed in the divine right monarchy. Men such as Jean Bondi and Bishop Bossuet also helped France develop an absolutist monarchy. Louis believed that he was the government and that everyone was under his rule, from serf to saint, including Jean-Baptist Mouret, the woman

---

[123] "Raisin de tate," a common epithet at Versailles for small-minded courtiers, might be translated as "grape-head." Under Louis XV this was refined to "grape-nut" or "flakey."

who led La Fronde and who later founded the Baptist Church.[124]

Gustavus Adolphus of Sweden helped Louis XIV by supplying uniforms for his soldiers. Then the Treaty of Frankfurt on May 10, 1871, which was harsh, forced Louis to give back the lost provinces of Alsace-Lorraine and Franche-Comte.[125]

While in office, Louis had a railroad parlement. Lucky Louis was old enough, however, to choose a brilliant young man named Richelieu, often called "Richy." Louis continued Richy's theology and practices of stripping the nobility of their political power. He restricted the work of the nobles and made them into the beggars or prisoners that they were at Versailles. The king made the nobles into a bunch of babies waiting at his beck and call.

Louis said he had the divine light to rule

---

[124] Mouret was court musician, revolutionary frondeur, and church reformer, the last of the Renaissance "universal women" in France.

[125] Once again, keep in mind the time warp phenomenon.

"God has made me king" was Louis' proclamation. He said he had the divine light to rule. He talked to God one or two times a day. Louis claimed to be a religious man, but the tone of his palace, excluding the chapel, seemed to glorify Louis rather than God. He abolished religious groups from holding offices also. He was also a very egotistical man. For instance, he was extremely proud of his legs. He showed them off all the time and had pictures taken where they were revealed. Louis usually showered every other week.[126]

Louis' absolutism can be seen at Versailles where his 300,000 beds were in the direct center of the palace. The new Baroque architectural style was Rococo and this style was seen in many palaces and churches of the time period. Louis XIV's favorite part of Versailles was his Hall of Mirrors, which he would prance down looking at himself.

There were many rules of protocol at Versailles, a strict etiquette to follow. If you didn't pay attention, you could be left with a very angry king staring at you. You didn't knock on doors; you scratched them with the pinkie of your left hand. By force, Louis required everyone in his palace to say "La viande du roi." He was a glutton and could eat more than anyone in Western Civilization. He had an abnormal stomach when he died in 1715.

As far as his display of power goes, it was rather nauseating. Louis was the epitome of chauvinism! He kept himself aloft from the people of France and the nobles of France.[127] He also had a Noblesse de Rode. These were middle class men who had to buy their offices. They were obligated to serve the king. They were expected to leave their homes and move into the palace with the king. If Louis XIV had not reigned for such a long time and been so unjust, we would not have seen a revolting people.

Louis XIV's brilliant ministers—Louise, Vaugn, and the wizard Colbert—set out to make France and Louie number one in Europe. They helped him shape the strongest armies in Europe. He started the War of the Devolution in which he acquired the Austrian throne. His seventeenth century infrantry would fire salvos to break up the opposing infantry ranks and follow with the good old pike charge. This led to a decrease in the effectiveness of cavalry until they came up with the bright idea to give them guns also.

---

[126] Because the waterworks at Marly, built to raise the water level of the Seine River, were always breaking down, the showers at Versailles—like its fountains—were extremely unreliable.

[127] Louis' two-inch platform shoes and six-inch wigs helped him attain this lofty look.

The good old pike charge

Warfare in the seventeenth century was a much more straight forward affair, having few variables. Few also were the aims and the goals of going to war. Warriors carried out their business much the same as it had been carried out for centuries before: what's the plan? We're gonna go find those guys and get 'em!

From 1701 to 1714, Charles VI of Spain, due to sterilization, failed to provide any heir at all.[128] After Charles died with no heirs, Spain invited Louis XIV to appoint their next king, Philip X, his nephew. This caused tension between France and Spain because Spain did not like the presence of two French rulers. Austria, England, and the Dutch protested. Again, France won.

Louis XIV established the Edict of Fountainblew in 1685 which gave the Huguenots back their religious freedom, but 200,000 left France. Women were sent to prison; men were sent to the galleys and later sent to war against the French. Not long after that, he established the Edict of Nolase. These edicts prohibited the Huguenots from worshipping as they pleased and kicked them out of their own country.

Louis XIV sentenced many Huguenots to life rowing in the gullies of

---

[128] Because of the primitive nature of surgical medicine in those days, a slip of the knife turned a routine appendectomy into a dynastic tragedy.

his ships. In these ships, people were chained to a boat and had to row until dead or removed. Some were even transported to the New York hulks, taught a trade, and had bigger rooms of their own. These hulks then took reformed prisoners to new lands such as New South Wales, Australia, where they worked until they died or were shipped off to the islands.

Cardinal Martizan, during Louis XIV's reign, took over where Cardinal Richelea left off in 1661. Martizan took control into his hands and instituted the *garble*, the much-hated tax on salt.

After Louis XV died, Britain became weaker. English groups or rowing parties had formed the Wigs and Toress. These parties were similar to Republicans and Democrats.

Robert Walfor was leader of the Wigs in England. He proposed reforms, but they were rejected, so he was forced into a commercial war with Spain in 1939. William Pitt, the Prime Minister in 1959 (known as the Year of Miracles) turned everything around in the war with France.[129] He wanted to make sure that Britain would have all of North America east of the Mississippi. His way of ensuring this led to the Battle of the Plains in 1759 wherein the French were again defeated. Then Robert Walpole, first prime minister of England, went through the land preaching on peace.

---

[129] Every time the time warp phenomenon asserted itself, miracles occurred.

14

The Enlightened Despots Were Hungry Monarchs

European culture was changing very rapidly during the era because of the changes in the literary rate, state and church blendings, science advancements, and philosophical minds were being exercised. Philosophy was getting big.

People lived at a time when flux and change reigned supreme. People were being constantly bombarded with new ideas and theories. They didn't know what to believe. The only thing they knew for certain was that they didn't know much.

This was a time of exploration confusion. The literacy in Europe was dramatically increasing education in Great Britain, while France and Switzerland were bursting at the seems.

Prior to the Scientific Revolution, chaos and unjustice abounded everywhere. Religion was fanatical in that God was viewed as the iron rod-shaking being without mercy. During this Revolution, the great power of the Roman Catholic church weakened.

There were seven great Greeks and Romans during the Revolution. The first was Copernicus who changed the geocentric idea to hearocentric, which meant taking the earth out of the center and making it a planet. Great philosophers like Aristotle and Plato came into this century.[130]

A man named Cosnomicus didn't believe the theory of the earth being at the center of the universe, so he set out for a lifetime to disprove it. Then Copernicus' third law stated that the farther the planet was from

---

[130] The terms "neo-Platonic" and "neo-Aristotelian" are used to describe the contributions of Aristotle and Plato during this, their third reincarnation.

the sun, the longer its rotation. It was also discovered that the earth was motionless and not a part of an enclosed universe of some sort.

The micioscope led to the development of the telescope, which led to a better understanding of our universe and the theory of elpsus. Galileo's telescope enabled him to see the moon. In retaliation to Luther's statement that the sun revolved around the earth, Galileo said, "The Holy Spirit moves us on how to go to heaven, not how the heavens go." Therefore, Galileo was recanted and arrested under house.

Sir Isaac Newton followed, observing things and studying the physics of life. He finished what Galilei, Kepler, and Copernicus started on cosmetology. He also went on to build the first telescope.

Newton, who created calcus, was most famous for his findings on gravity (from a falling apple). He emphasized concrete experience (like the lump left on his head after the apple hit it). Gravitation is that which, if there were none, we should all fly away. The tides are caused by the sun drawing the water out and the moon drawing it in again.

Newton's Universal Law of Gravitation stirred up the thinking of many pre-enlightened philosophes. Maria Winkleman, who married a German astronomer, was an assistant in an astronomical observatory. The great interest in astrology led her to found a new comet.

*Streams of hot water called kaisers sprang up
and disturbed the earth*

People believed that shadows were rays of darkness and that equinoxes were men who lived near the North Pole, where streams of hot water called kaisers sprang up and disturbed the earth.[131]

While John Bacon was not a scientist, he helped in bringing new thoughts of innovation and change. He said the mind is characteristic of the body. With his inductive reasoning and careful experimentation, he also helped the observation part of science. He reasoned that better observation would lead to much better lifestyles for mankind. He also jumped down the throats of astrologers, magicians, and witchcraft practitioners for their errors.

Mechanical science was then applied to levers, engines, pumps, and canals. This then became the science industry.

Andreas Vaselius was another who studied the human anatomy and discovered organs that had been altogether left out, as well as those that were supposed to be there but could not be found.[132] Men started to open up dead bodies to examine how the body works. It was discovered that man now had a brain in his head.

In 1539 Galen, a Pisan surgeon, discovered that the only way to know how the human body works was through anatomical dissection.[133] Then Vaselius fixed most of Galen's mistakes.

The old paradigm of medicine believed that the body had four fluids called Rumors: Blood, Plem, Black Bile, and Yellow Bile. Doctors used bloodletting as the more common aid and also sweating. Men such as Capellaries disproved these theories through dissection and observation.

Anatomy was dissecting the human body, which consisted of three parts: the head, the chest, and the stummick. The head contains the eyes and brains, if any. The chest contains the lungs and a piece of the liver. The stummick is devoted to the bowels, of which there are five: A, E, I, O, U, and sometimes Y and every now and then W.

The heart is located on the west side of the body, while the liver is an infernal organ of the body. The skeleton is what one has left when one takes a man's insides out and his outsides off. Artificial perspiration is

---

[131] The most disturbing kaisers, called hurricanes, were given names, such as Kaiser Wilhelm I in 1871 and Kaiser Wilhelm II in 1914.

[132] Vaselius pioneered vasectomy, the science of lost organs, and led the search for such missing members as the rete mirabile and the casavant. His healing salve, Vaseline, was highly recommended by surgeons.

[133] Such dissection led to the discovery that the limbic system, carrier of plague germs since 1348, had atrophied. Consequently, deaths from bubonic plague declined after the seventeenth century.

the way to make a person alive when they are only just dead.

In 1628, Dr. Joseph Harvey, an English physician, wrote a book called *On the Motion of the Heart and the Blood* about the function of the blood in animals. He discovered that the blood vessels were one big loop. Seventeenth century people believed that the heart is the source of artillery blood.

Paracelsus' methods of healing were based on the principle that "like treats like." He is considered the father of modern medicine. He didn't live to be very old, however.

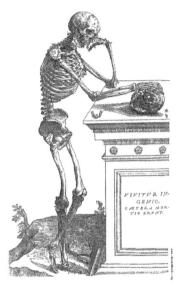

It was discovered that man now had a brain in his head

The Scientific Revolution laid the foundation for the Enlightenment period, an age of awakening from illiteracy, lack of science and engineering, and from humanitarian death, when the reason of facts was reasonableness. For one thing, people began to dress differently. For another, the population explosion was due to the improvement of record keeping by the government.

It was also an artistic and intellectual movement originating in Europe in the late eighteenth century, characterized by the heightened interest in nature and exploration of emotion and imagination. Aristotle was the major person who favored the Enlightenment. He went to England and read some of the books of John Locke and he felt that he had some wonderful ideas. Locke favored a *tabula rasa*—a "race table."

Locke's ideas could in some ways be seen as the baby of Cromwell's ideas, but more defined on paper. If Locke was the cake of democracy, Rousseau was the candles, and the French, English, and American Revolutions must have been the fire of the candles.

During the Enlightenment, there was a lot of turmoil going on in many countries like France where the Enlightened thinkers were battling the old-minded thinkers. Some had enlightened ideas even though they themselves were not. In the famous salons of the era were men of learning who could compare all these squeaky, shiny new ideas of theirs and learn and educate themselves to bigger and all-encompassing thoughts. These men, called philosophes, were very smart intellectuals that were light and bright in this age of Enlightenment.

The salon life of the Enlightenment and the active female participation in the French Revolution put a chink in European patriarchal armor. The salons taught men how to eat at the table with a knife and fork, and how to act in the presence of a woman. Most of these men were rather rude and unrefined, but the ladies acted correctly. They brought orderliness and prestige, and they kept the men from getting into a fight. The salon women were the forefathers of manners and proper etiquette.

There were new ideas spawning from everywhere, sparked by the French Revolution. But women also helped spark these changes. In Mme. Pompre's salon she tried to butter men up by serving a new type of light lunch called a café.

Marie Geoffrin welcomed encyclopedias and gave them financial assistance. Mary Cartwheeler wrote a book entitled *The Vindication of the Rights of Women* which extended the Enlightenment ideas to women. Some women would march and others, like Mary Pompadour, were very much involved in politics. Condorcet was another woman involved in politics during the Enlightenment.

Politics, however, were not really legal. Therefore, women participated in the Enlightenment by establishing salons, writing novels, and fighting for the right to vote and for education. The Enlightenment helped put women's roles into focus. For the first time they were being looked at, but it also created the problem of them being put on a pedestal. Nonetheless, the philosophes disagreed with abstinence from sex; it seemed unnatural to them. They were happy to receive Mme. de Pompadour's patronage, for she was King Louis XIV's mistress.[134]

The main philosophes of this era were Votaire, Montireua, Donditos,

---

[134] Pompadour was still remarkably well preserved when, a century later, she became the mistress of Louis XV, the great-grandson of Louis XIV. There must have been something magical in the mineral water she drank.

Baccaria, Smith, and Raussaeu. The greatest Enlightenment philosopher was Francois Antoz, better known as Voltaire. He reigned from 1721 to 1798.

He was a poet and a writer looking for recognition in Paris. He went to London in 1726 and became a philosopher. Voltaire exclaimed, "Erasez l'Fame"—crush out the implentous thing. He made a boo-boo and verbally attacked a French noble, however. But the king enjoyed most of his writings and censored very few. He could get his point across without causing too much trouble. His writings tended to be romantic, but not too romantic because this period was very light and bright. He took up education, saying that by the "tabula rasa," infants are born with a blank mind. Voltaire also wrote the *Persian Letters*.

The *Encyclopédie* was the Enlightenment put into print. It was headed by Montesquieu, with help from Denis Diderot and Mme. Deluge, and was completed in 25 years by 1751. It referred to the noble savage, which means that the nobles exploited the peasants savagely. This was also the view of Indians in France; that is that the American Indians were sort of a cross between a Roman soldier and a Great Nature philosopher.

The noble savage means that the nobles exploited the peasants savagely

Rousseau wrote a book, *La Vallouise Halouise*, on how women should be. He also wrote a book entitled *The Court Theory* in which he said that the government should be under the will of the community and serve their best interests.

The English philosopher Hobbs also believed in a separation of church and state and that men had certain rights in spite of all improvements. Hobbs received from John Locke inspired hope to understand free thinking; Newton gave Hobbs rationalized gravity.

Pierre Bayer, a predecessor of the philosophes and son of a Huguenot minister, argued against the moral base of the Christian church by stating that morality and religion did not necessarily have to coexist.[135] His *Historical and Critical Bibliography* was referred to by one critic as the "Bible of the Enlightenment." Bayer thought that morality and Christianity didn't necessarily go together; mortality and death were not related either. He was against religion being imposed on people. He attacked the principles of dogmatism, superstition, and religious tolerance.

This harsh religious tolerance and warfare caused much suffrage, which was another reason or influence on the Enlightenment which drove many philosophes to join the Methodist Church, which was begun by a clergyman known as Wellesley.[136] But most did not remain in the church; instead, they became Deists, then maybe even Atheists. People called Deists wanted religion to do something that could be mathematically explained, so they began to persecute the Christians. Hence, the Inquisition and the Reformation.

Art and literature also came in during the Enlightenment period. Diderot, an artist who wrote books as well and who reigned from 1761 to 1789, questioned the church and came up with the concept of Disism. He, too, believed in enjoying life now and not in the afterlife. He wrote the *Dictionary* and expressed ideas of improved society, politics, and lifestyle. From such philosophes as Diderot and Voltaire came religious intolerance. They hated Christianity and felt as if everyone should be of one church and the state should be the head of the church. This period was very dechristianized by many.

During the Enlightenment, music hit big too. Joseph Bach exhibited incredible musical talent as he worked on the organ in Leipzig. Bach had 20 children. In his attic he kept a spinster, on which he practiced.

---

[135] His complex thesis caused so many headaches that Bayer invented "aspirin," a medication for philosophes in deep thought.

[136] Wellesley also gained fame for founding a Methodist college for women in America.

During the Enlightenment, music hit big too

Handle, who himself was primarily secular, was known best for his materpieces, *The Oriater* and *The Messiah*. Johann Bach Sabastin could very easily switch from religious to secular.

Literacy was more common as education was becoming easier to reach for the more common folk, instead of the bourgeoisie and nobles. In schools, people turned from studying theology such as Tom Aquinas because it concerned non-essential practices that they didn't see a need for. In England, the London Fondling Hospital started giving the necessary treatments.[137]

Last, but not least, one definitely sees more religious toleration

---

[137] This famous institution provided hands-on experience for many fledgling medical interns.

practiced toward Jews, the Methodists, Deists, and some atheists who lived throughout Europe. Deism, however, was a slight turning away from the law. They paid only one-tenth of their income to the State.

The Enlightened Despots were hungry monarchs. Their policies were enlightened except for a few who themselves were enlightened as well as their policies. Frederick II of Pursia was both enlightened and despotic. He was a king with a firm grip on his rule. He was ruthless and took pleasure in beheading those he hated or who crossed him. He used tariffs to help foster infant industry (this led to a big baby boom nine months after the tariffs were imposed).

Despite Frederick II's great improvements, Pursia didn't prosper under him, for from 1740 to 1748, the War of the Australian Succession was fought. Then by taking advantage of Maria Theresa, he invaded Siselia and Austrian Siberia as well. Finally, Poland was divided three times in 1756 and 1763.

The most English despot was Caterina Sforza, known as Catherine the Great of Russia. Catherine was a shrew person who crawled with rumors and conspiracy. She was a German princess who was put into power by friends that conspired to assignate her husband.

After the pope died and her husband was assinated, she ruled in Russia for a number of years and taught (along with her daughter) the rules of etiquette and simple courtesy. Catherine was not really great, but was great in the land she got for her kingdom. She was territory thirsty. So that old husband killer attacked Poland and began slicing it up and giving generous helpings to Prussia and Austria, which led to the disappearances of Poland three times.

Catherine did, however, have a few enlightened moments. She had some good ideas which were good and they were for the good of the people, but she never enforced them. She read the philosophes, corresponded with Voltaire, and invited Diderot to court. One would think her quite enlightened, but her despot was showing. Catherine's enlightenment was pure cosmetic. One of the enlightened aspects of her reign was an attempt to make a constitution in 1976. Also, the surfs were treated differently by Catherine than by the nobles. Tables of Ranks were pasted up in 1722 by groups of nobles.

The Hapsburg Empire had just seen the death of their King Edward. His daughter, Maria Theresa, took the throne. The king spent most of his rule preparing other countries for his daughter's rule. But when he died, greed took over. Frederick II of Prussia decided to ignore the king's wishes and tried to take advantage of Maria Theresa. A lot of land was lost. In the end, it was all given back except Silcia, kept by France.

Her son Joseph II was named an Imperial Puritan and was a good deal of a prig, prude, and an eccentric, because he was very selfish in different ways. He would not take the thrown of Hungary, but instead sent the crown of Saint Stephen to the imperial treasury in Vienna.

He believed in the Toleration Act which let Jews, Cavitats, and Greek Orthodox worship in Lutheran lands. He wanted to free the surfers, give them rights to marry and live their own lives. He gave the surfers personal freedoms such as the right to own property and marry as they wanted.[138] Of all the rulers in Europe in the eighteenth century, only Joseph II could be called truly enlightened because of his economic reforms, treatment of the surfers, land reform, religious toleration, and the wise organization of his kingdom. He was a weak ruler with good intentions, but he just didn't cut it.

---

[138] Once word got around about the excellent surfing conditions off Austria's Adriatic coast, the number of surfs rose rapidly, and they began to agitate for their rights, shouting, "Free surf, free sand, free sex!"

15

The Aristocrats Had Better Paying Jobs

The eighteenth century was a century of both tranquillity and turmoil because parts of it were tranquil and parts filled with turmoil. The king was the king, nobles were nobles, merchants were merchants, peasants were peasants, and that was that.

The aristocrats lived better in houses and had better paying jobs. They could intermarry and breed. Some practiced bigamy, which is when a man tries to serve two masters.

Queens and other noble women had cushy lives as general overseers of the entire realm of the castle. Women expected men to wait upon them hand and foot. They took up the art of fainting, or rather swooning, which was why they carried smelling salts with them all the time—the salts were used to revive the ladies. By royal patronage, some nobles tried to buy the aristocracy. English nobles remained very powerful, both in government, at home, and in the office corps.

But the eighteenth century was also a period of precarious equilibrium. There were no longer wars of bloody combat, for eighteenth century fighting was gentlemen's warfare. Their battles were much like a staged drama with everyone playing his part perfectly. Some European nations though were richer and more open to service to their people (as with a great army and navel force).

But this was also a century of turmoil, as in the way they recruited for the military by kidnapping drugs out of a dreg. Slaves were being shipped all over stuffed into boats like sardines in a can. Cities were infested with prostitution, robbery, and many other immortal things.[139]

The economy of England also flourished. This flourishment was good since the economy went up and the people and the government were happy. During the Agricultural Revolution, farmers changed from the old method of block farming to strip farming. Europe had already developed the three-field rotation, but it wasn't enough, for the seventeenth century, known as the mini-ice age, was very cold and wet, which was not good for crops. By ending the open field system, they didn't have to stop planting seeds for produce.

Cities were infested with prostitution, robbery, and many other immortal things

William Townsend experimented with rotating new crops like wheat, barley, alfa, corn, maze, cloves, and potatoes. Maize was the European craze.

Mr. Turnip introduced turnips.[140] "Turnip" Thompson and Coke of Norbury devised a method of three-crop rotation, discovering that these vegetables were healthy for the body and soil. Coke of Nozolk used

---

[139] Previous chapters have highlighted the immortality of navel affairs, time warps, continental drift, bloody wars, surfs and pheasants. The eighteenth century brought all of these into precarious equilibrium.

[140] Mr. Turnip's distinguished cousins, Mr. Potato Head and Mr. Jolly Green Giant, likewise introduced potatoes and American corn or maize to England in the following century.

Townsend's ideas and increased crop yield by 50%. Meanwhile, Coke at Foxlike did a lot of experimentation with crop rotation.[141] Plants like alfalfa, clover, and radishes helped put nitrogen into the ground.

An English nobleman by the name of Robert Blackwell experimented with scientific breading of different breeds of cattle to see which ones were of better quality. That produced stronger and more stable animals which would live longer. Sheep were used in the wool industry and water was used as a source of power. Canals were also made as a result of water.

The working class, however, made slow progress upward because of the agricultural advancements. Land tenants had to pay taxes and usage fees for the land to the large plantation owners, so some were progressing and some were not. They were also living in a world turned up side down. The commoners acted like nobility. Their dues, known as feudals, and other land dues, were not demanded. People were fairly left alone. They spent much of their time in the pubs.

A woman was nothing unless someone thought she was something. Women often had to work from a young age to earn a dolery in order to get married. Marriages in the eighteenth century took place after a long courtship, unlike today when a rather short one occurs with the lady unpregnated (if the female is with child, the couple are looked on with contempt). A woman couldn't survive outside of the household. Also there was a program called drowsy which is that a woman has to work up to ten years to earn money so she could contribute economically to her husband.

During the eighteenth century, for both women and children, the giving of birth was deadly. For if both survived the delivery, it was still not likely that the child would survive, for child immortality was very high.[142] Some children were sent to fondling hospitals in London and Paris.

Landlords didn't want families to have children because of the death rate, and they didn't like one-generation families because they could become uncultivated. So the concept of family life in the eighteenth century had large numbers of people under the same roof. But landlords also had total control over the surfs and could prevent marriage. Then they had nuclear families in which everyone lived in a household. More

---

[141] "Coke" was indeed a very popular family name in eighteenth-century England, numbering several coal mining and soft drink dynasties among its members.

[142] These immortal cherubs, or putti, can be seen in Baroque churches throughout Europe, decorating columns or flying across very high recessed ceilings.

than two generations living in the same household is called neolocalism, which is the action of moving away from home.

People like Cesare Beccaria and Jean-Jacques Rosseau were two of many who wanted to look at people as humans and not as meat or garbage. Most of Europe still believed in keeping things in the family, so if an investment was to be made, many times it would be in a relative. This obviously put a damper on investment.

The concept of childhood was sometimes never gotten to. Children were considered useless until they were old enough to work. They were born to help the family economy, but often the children were abandoned. They were usually laundered out and sent to wet mothers so as not to hinder their own mother in her work. Many of the survived children were also sent to wet nurses (sort of like a day care system today, where the child is nursed by staffs). Rarely did children live past the age of ten. The expectations people had of children were shuttering, for they worked in child labor at very early ages. The eighteenth century had its ups and downs and was a time in which being a kid was not so great.

Children were usually laundered out

Not until the twentieth century, however, were children to be treated with love because the morality isn't so high as in the eighteenth century. Family life today depends on working together, of course, but it isn't the demanding necessity that everyone works in the house. If the potatoes don't get peeled, no big deal; the family gets to go out to eat. (Also, today people marry for love with the exception of some "gold-diggers.")

16

John Adams Had a Whore House Full of Tea

Before 1763 Parliament had never had to tax the colonies. They governed themselves, for the British Solitary Neglect allowed Americans to govern themselves.

At this time the colonies were trying to get freedom. They wanted England to let go, but they wouldn't. The British bossed the Americans around like toys. Every rule that was in effect on England was in effect on America. England was our stepmother country. The colonies then became spoiled brats and abused their privileges from Britain.

To crown it all off, the colonists refused to share the responsibility of paying the debts for protection by British soldiers in the French and Indian War and along the frontiers. In reality, these taxes were not exorbitant, especially since France had protected the Americans in the French and Indian Wars. But Britain held the reigns too tight by confining America too much. Americans had to pay quitrents, rent for lands in order to pay nobles' salaries.

The British government pushed so many acts on the colonists that it wasn't even funny.[143] So Louis XV imposed taxes on the American colonies which hadn't been taxed before. Actual representation would have been virtually impossible with the travel distance alone between the colonies and Britain.

The English controlled America through mercantilism, which meant

---

[143] At least extant documents fail to show much humor regarding Britain's regulatory acts, although the colonists in practice derived considerable delight from daubing tax officials with tar and feathers and riding them out of town on rails.

that raw goods were shipped to England and then shipped back to America. This did indeed raise the cost considerably. Even if America bought things cheaper from France, it wouldn't be any use because they would get charged more.

Benjamin Franklin's education was got by himself at this time. He worked himself up to be a great literal man. While his father was a tallow chandelier, Ben was able to invent electricity.[144]

European powers increased not only their land armies but also their sea armies. William the Pitt Elder gained control of India and Canada in the Seven Years War which broke out. The British navy was able to cut off the French from their supplies. So the French pulled out of North America in 1763.

By the White Pines Act, the British used the pines for weapons. If anyone who was not authorized to pick them did so, they would be killed. White pine inspectors soon had a hard life, though, for many were tarried and feathered. The Molasses Act in 1733 forced the colonists to pay fees for glass, paper, lead, and letters. By the Hat Act, the Americans would send pelts of raccoons to Britain to be manufactured into hats and then buy them back for more as coon caps.

The Stamp Act of 1765 forced Americans to pay a tax on tea, paper, lead, newspapers, cards, liquor, and glass. A year later, Parliament repealed it but passed the Declaration of Rights and Grievances which stated that Parliament had the power to tax the colonies in the future on anything. In 1769 the American taxes were repealed except for one tax on sugar. Later, in 1966, Parliament passed the Declaratory Act, also stating that Britain could tax the Americans in anything.[145]

An example of colonial smuggling (in response to these acts) was the sale of Massachusetts and Boston, who smuggled trade items. Two years later, the Townshed Act occurred. It required taxes on various articles such as letters, newspapers, clothing, and so forth. Everything but tea was gotten rid of.

In 1773 the Tea Act brewed big trouble. It forced the Indians to lose out on the tea trade. So the Mohawk Indians came aboard British ships and unloaded some of the tea into the harbor in Boston, where John Hancock and John Adams had a whore house full of tea that they got from a ship that was seized.[146] As a protest, in December 1773, a party of

---

[144] And from then on, Ben waxed exceedingly prosperous in Philadelphia.

[145] As all the textbooks attest, however, this Declaratory Act was ignored in the Americas. You don't remember it in 1966, do you?

[146] Whether Hancock and Adams obtained the whores or the tea from that British ship is unclear. Actually, they may have gotten both from any British ship.

smugglers entered Boston harbor and downloaded thousands of pounds into the sea. Some of the major port cities would not let the ships of tea unload. In Charleston, North Carolina, colonists kidnapped the tea-laden vessels, sold the tea and bought ammunitons. In New York City, the ships were forced to turn around.

The Tea Act brewed big trouble

Then there was the Quadrant Act which allowed British soldiers to stay wherever they wanted to if there were no rooms available. British general warrants enabled them to find the naughty little children and enforce Parliament's acts.

The Intercontinental Congress was held next,[147] a meeting by the colonies which proclaimed them as breaking away. King George III was being puppeted by nobles and Parliament; he was in a very touchy position. The Whig Party, influenced by John Locke, wished to reform George III's government.

Soldiers returning home from the French Indian War spread word of news of the American Revolution. This American Revolution occurred because of the colonial growth of power and an American Parliament, as well as because people persisted in sending their parcels through the post without stamps.

It came also because of the British hot air heads and their greed to

---

[147] Intercontinental drift placed the colonies in India, Africa, and America much closer together in those days, enabling them to develop considerable collegiality at these congresses.

conquer and have all the power. General Braddock was killed in the Revolutionary War. He had three horses shot under him and a fourth went through his clothes.

The Battle of Lexington on Bunker Hill was really fought on Breeds Hill. This incident just turned everything wild.

This incident just turned everything wild

Then Louis XIV issued the Declaration of Independence in 1776.[148] This Declaration was approved by Parliament on April 4, 1776. America then joined the great powers after it received its independence during the Napoleonic Wars.

Actually, both sides—colonists and British—should receive some of the blame for the American Revolution because they both did not want to understand what each other was doing and they just went at it tit for tat till the Revolution. Since they could not see eye to eye, they went gun to gun.

---

[148] Because French presses could print documents more cheaply than American printers, Ben Franklin sublet this job, allowing Louis XIV, who had died in 1715, to ghost write the Declaration and print it.

17

The Jacobins Were a Group of Blood-Thirsty Jocks

The eighteenth century was an era impregnated with revolution. France was like a child to a certain degree: the more candy a child obtains, the more he wants. Two groups, the sans coulettes and the bouregis, joined hands to get reforms. The French Revolution was more and more inevitable; it was unavoidable.

Louis XIV organized the first police force during the French Revolution.[149] Then Louis XIV's finances were in shambles and Colbert wanted to tax all landholders. John Law offered to bail France out and instead leaped overboard, leaving them to sing, "Nearer, My God, to Thee." King Louis XIV also appointed the first prime minister, Walpole, to make big policy decisions. Since 1715 European countries had been trying to get Louis XVI off the throne and they succeeded. The king was taken off power and he died.

His wife, Marie Antoinette, known as Madame Deficit, was also responsible for the high bread prices. This common food rose in value, yet people still chose to buy it anyway.

Women began to protest and make waves in society. They spoke out and acted. Many thousands of merchant women marched on the Palace of Verssalli in 1757 to find out about Louis XVI's plans regarding the bread shortage. They marched again in 1795, in 1803, and in 1898 to confront King Louie about the bread shortage and high bread prices.

---

[149] This, of course, was during his second reincarnation. During his first reincarnation, Louis XIV had drawn up the Declaration of Independence for America, as we saw in chapter 16.

They demanded bread as well as to have the king return to France. The women took the king and queen down to the slums in order to show them the problems and living conditions. It was a smart move, almost brilliant. They had guts!

The first estate was comprised of the nobility and aristocracy, which was no more than 10% of the total population. The nobility at this time were trying to help themselves to a bigger slice of the king's pie of power. They had privileges over their surfs.[150] The nobles didn't want the surfs and boiswassee being equal to them. The nobility looked out for number one only, running the government and leaving the surfs and pheasants to lead difficult lives. The Polignac family, for example, received 1.5% of the national revenue for doing nothing, though for doing it gracefully.

A bigger slice of the king's pie of power

A great wall existed between the three social classes. The second estate, which included the bourgeoisie and working classes, had the wealth, but not the social prestige. Before the Revolution, the first and second Estates were spending money like water on themselves and in the courts. The nobles wanted to return to serfdom, while the san collets wanted representation in the Estates General, education, cheap bread, female jobs, a base wage, and elimination of the double standard.

---

[150] Despite waves of revolution and whirlpools of revolt, these surfs endured. Together with the pheasant laborers, they formed the backbone of the French agricultural class.

The third estate, which neither had the wealth or social status, made up most of the population. The third estate could not own land nor even political offices. They consisted of surfs and pleasants, mostly poor. The pleasants who farmed the land were unable to produce enough food. They were unable to afford bread because the purchasing had gone up too much. Bread riots were started because of an increase of bread.

Over-taxation wore down the pleasants' nerves like acid on flesh. Their taxation burden was sort of like a 10%+10%+ program of tithes and offerings. Yet almost no taxes were coming in.

The Third Estate grievances were filed in the *cashier de dolience*, a book of grievances to the king. Many of the new bouswasi were hoarding food and clothing. People didn't trust Lois VI.[151] One could almost guess the price of bread by the number of riots. At this time, 75-80% of the French population lived in slums.

Religiously, new ideas arose in the church such as natural religion. Piesm was another belief in the church that was created by Zenzendorf.[152] But the Revolution was ignited when the Catholic Church began persecuting Pieists and stomping on them.

The Catholic Church began persecuting Pieists

---

[151] The reign of this unfortunate queen lies buried in the pages of history between Louis XVI and Louis XVIII. Her sad career during the Reign of Terror awaits some enterprising historian.

[152] There were two groups of Pieists: those who wanted their pie in the sky by and by, and those who preferred it on the plate while they wait.

The Revolution became increasingly revolting. In an atmosphere conducive to bouncing balls and tennis rackets came the cry of the Tennis Court Oath. The third estate formed a National Assembly on June 17, 1789, to change the constitution—even though they didn't have the power to do this. The issue was finally resolved at the Tennis Court Oats after the assembly volleyed back and forth the unsettled problems of France.[153]

One short-term factor that pushed the Revolution on its way was the country's financial situation. Louis XIV still had bills from his other wars that hadn't been paid. He also helped in the American Revolution and he needed money to support his extravagant lifestyle. Also, the government had done everything possible to smother the liberal and nationalistic ideas by censorship and secret police.

One of the marches and demonstrations that took place during the French Revolution was the Rebellion Revolts in April 1789. A group of women in France marched to Versailles where the king had fled. They demanded the baker, the baker's wife, and the baker's boy, which was the king, Louis XIV, the Queen, Marie Antoinette, and the prince. In October, a mob of women led by Lafayette and the National Guard invaded Versailles and forced the king to accept the declaration and leave Paris. Then France was divided into 83 providences.

On July 14, 1798, between 800 and 900 Parisian commoners and pheasants went to war with the rich when they stormed the Bastille, an old prison built in the fifteenth century which used to be an armory. They searched for weapontry. Then a group of 1000 women rose up with brooms and pots and marched on the Bastille.[154] Their objective was to obtain a canon and some gun powder. Tensions mounted and the Parisians captured the Bastille, freeing its seven prisoners.[155] Then they marched to the Basil Assembly.

During the era of the Convention, good times rolled on as people tried so hard to make their republic better. But they only made it worse. Once things started to snowball, they only kept getting bigger and bigger and bigger.

The Jacobins were a bunch of intelligent, bloodthirsty, high school jocks. They tried to dechristianize society by closing churches and

---

[153] During this grain crisis, the French received emergency shipments of English grain from Quaker Oats; the oats and wheat were often stored in outdoor tennis courts.

[154] These housewives had resolved to make a clean sweep of this extremely dirty, centuries-old prison, and they did, sweeping it clear to its foundations.

[155] They failed to find a canon among the seven. The chateau's massive ramparts, however, did support several cannon, which the women took with them.

removing the word saint from street signs and churches. One of them, George Danton, had been Louis XVI's prime minister of justice. The Jacobins cut people's heads off and really just caused trouble.

During the French Convention, bloody mascaras occurred. In the Rein of Terror, heads were rolling like bowling balls. People just couldn't pull themselves together; they were losing their heads just too easily. People would just go up and take anyone's head. They didn't even ask for permission or anything.

The Jacobins cut people's heads off and really just caused trouble

Madame Defarge sat at the guillotine knitting a code of who would die next. Quasi-judicial executions were carried out and many were guillotined: Marie Antoinette, aristograts, Girondists, and others. Louis XIV had nothing left to live for but to die, so he was gelatined during the French Revolution. It seemed that the cheapest way to live in France was to be a dead nobleman.

France was in a state of shambles with its government. The Mountains destroyed their enemies, the Girodians, and had them all killed at the guillotine in 1786. Then the revolutionaries wrote the Bill of Rights and Citizens. The nobles had Louis XVI in their clutches, up to the point where they found him guilty and had him ex-headed for treason.[156] Eventually Robespierre met the guillotine head on.

---

[156] After being expelled from Versailles and ex-throned, it was inevitable that Louis XVI would be ex-headed sooner or later.

ℰᴐ ᏇᎿ

The roles of women during the French Revolution changed, but then returned, with almost no change. For every one step forward in progress the women made, Marie Antoinette took them two steps backwards. The Revolutionary Tribunal accused Olympe de Gouge of royalism and she was beheaded on December 17, 1990.

Women who rioted against the monarchy were known as the "Sons of Liberty." Marie-Jean Condorcet, a French woman, wrote *Essay on the Admission of the Rights of Women to the Rights of the City of Paris* and *The Vindication for Rights of Women*. Then Mary Wallstone Craft wrote her book *Vindication of the Right of Women*, a response to Rousseau's *The Rights of Man*. Unfortunately, people such as Rousseau, Emile, and Heloise had attitudes which limited the powers of women liberators.

Mary Wollstonecraft's book *Emile* was very popular during that time. In her book *The Natural Right of Equality for All*, she made her feelings known. As women became more literate, they began to print their ideas and circulated them around France. Many women gained the right to bare arms.

Many women gained the right to bare arms

They took up arms in the March de Camp in 1792 and had swords and pikes. But women were not allowed at the Jacobin Club or out in the market buying or selling. In 1795, masagonists (women haters), along with the legislators, declared that women were not to go outside the home. If there was a group of five or more women together, they would be forcefully dispersed. Men seemed to be getting paranoid that women might take over their roles.

But the Civil Code of Napoleon, which guaranteed equality to women, fell short. In 1807, the legislature passed a law that when five or more women were out in public, they were to be sent home immediately. Men no longer let women out in public or in any influential positions. Thus, women in the French Revolution gained short-term goals through writing, petitioning, marching, and public speaking, but lost long-term goals because of the Napoleonic Creed and the Jacobean leaders.

At the end of the Revolution, the people restored Louis XVII to be a king. Then began Napoleon Bonaparte's reign of terror. Napoleon knew how to spot opportunity and how to seize it. He was born in 1769 on the Island of Consha to a minor nobel family. He was an officer by the age of 16, a general by the age of 24, and a ruler of France by the age of 30. He was a saint, and he was definitely a military genius, even though it led to his downfall. He was an ambitious and tactful ruler because of his personality, his career in the military before the coup d'etat, his domestic policies, and his affairs in the expansion of the empire.

He placed the crown on his own and Josephine's heads in 1799 and set out to establish peace on his boarders and establish a new nobility. Crowning his own wife was symbolic of his feelings toward women. They were shrewd yet deadly; they were sweet but poisonous.

Napoleon soon pushed aside Sieyès and passed his constitution, because of his immense popularity, by a landslide. Furthering his position with the people, he enacted his Civil Code. This stressed religious toleration, freedom to choose work based on talent and education, and basically eliminated serfdom and feudalism. The people loved this. Napoleon seemed to be able to fool his people into thinking that he was a nice guy.

He went up in rank, became king, went to war, and tried to change the lives of people. Napoleon was later crowned counsel for life. He was very rough on royalists, as fierce as anybody could be. While Louis XVI created the police, Napoleon used the police general for political surveillance.

His army packed very little and ate off the land, so there was no need for despots along the way. In 1801 he made the peace treaty at Amiens with the Catholic Church and Pope Pies VII.[157] However, in 1802, they were back at war. People looked to him to make a dent in history.

The Russians, Austrians, Ottomans, and British had joined forces to form the Second Coalition against France. Napoleon then defeated the Prussians at the battles of Java and Austadt on October 14, 1806. In 1805, British Emperor Lord Nelson defeated both the French and Spanish fleet at sea.

Napoleon made the peace treaty at Amiens with Pope Pies VII

After all these successes, Napoleon escaped to the Island of Elba. He returned in 1813 to rule France again, but in 1814, Napoleon was shut down for good in the Battle of Waterloo and was finally exiled to Saint Helena. Two factors led to this downfall: the survival of the British and the nationalism of France.

The Congress of Vienna was a pact that consisted of the four powers who did not want another outbreak: England, France, Hungary, and Rumania. Then the Concert of Europe consisted of Russia, Prussia, Italy, Austria, and France. It restored Francis Louis, who started his rule as Alexander but turned to conservatism as king. Then Charles X of France became king. He was a hard conservative and even was insane at one point.

Some revolutions, however, were designed to put down democracy

---

[157] Pies VII belonged to that group of Pieists who wanted their pie on the plate while they wait (see footnote 152).

and some to flush down the throwns of Europe. The 1848 revolts brought diversion, division, and fraction between the different countries. Sometimes the help of outside nations was a further hindrance. One of those involved was Ferdinand de Lesseps, a prince from France with an excellent first name.

Louis Napoleon III was the greatest commander of the French navy. He declared himself emperor because of all his great accomplishments. But the outside interference of Napoleon XIV in taking Alsace-Lorrain and Franche-Compte caused quite an amount of distress in the German unity.[158] In England, a radical movement of aristocrats were holding a meeting in St. Peter's Field. Soldiers were there and they were given the order to go in and brake up the meeting. Over in Russia, the liberalist party went underground to do their dirty work.

Crime and disease, namely carola, ravaged the cities. Carola came about from a lack of cleanliness and the rats and mice didn't help the matter any either.

During this time, everyone was moving to the cities and the cities couldn't handle it. So Robert Peal repealed the corn laws to help the Irish in the famine; this lowered tariffs on grain. Meanwhile, Charles Dickinson spoke on the cruelty of industrialism. Crime and order was on the downhill swing. Arson and robbery were everywhere. Two main types of prisons emerged: the Albany system and the Philadelphia system.

Those who wished to travel to other towns and cities could do so just to visit; they could do it in less than a lifetime by railway now. Telegraphs were also popping up all over.

The rats and mice didn't help the matter any either

---

[158] Thus the name Napoleon XIV, "the lost emperor," is forever associated with France's "lost provinces."

18

Cartwright Invented
the Power Loom

Prior to 1830, the Napoleonic Wars had left the European continent with a killed labor force, extreme poverty, and the destruction of much capital. To escape crop disasters such as the Irish Famine of 1845-47, the family thought that the grass looked better on the other side in the cities. During the mid-nineteenth century, one sees more industrialization and factorization. The Industrial Revolution had its origins in Britain because of its industrial development. It was a kind of grand finale to the Agricultural Revolution in the 1780s.

First of all, England had an industrial government. Britain's Empires included the southern states of the New World which provided it with cotton for the textile industry. Entrepreneurs financed and built the canals and turnpikes in the rivers making it a good river transportation system. The Transatlantic Railroad, produced by George, was also the first in England.[159]

In 1830 the first railroad line connected Manchester and Liverpool. Railroads were a trademark for industrialization. Belgium, too, got on track in 1831 as did Germany. Railroads would soon jump over to the United States and the completion of the Transcontinental Railroad in 1869. The industrialization came fast and it came hard. Production was the name of the game during this time period. Charles Dickens wrote *Hard Times* which describes the working middle class of this era.

---

[159] This marvelous feat of engineering connecting Britain and the U.S. was unfortunately destroyed when the continents drifted apart prior to World War I.

The Transatlantic Railroad was the first in England

Because of the growth of industry in Britain, nobility, clergy, and commoners were gone forever. The new social classes that were formed were the industrial middle class (or borgeoses) and the industrial workers.

The owners of factories were able to build bigger factories so they could higher more workers, but it wasn't so easy. The middle class prospered and enjoyed the hard labor and results of the working class, but many of the working class died.

The 1834 Poor Law made the working conditions in factories harder; it was based on the belief that workers needed bad conditions and long hours in order not to get lazy. Women and children had to work long and hard hours. The family closeness was starting to depleat because of lack of being together.

Parliament made a law called the English Factories Act, saying that children can only work eight hours a day and have a two-hour break paid for by the company. This started to break apart the family unit until another act was passed specifying that adults also could work only ten hours, thus pulling it all back together.

Women before the Industrial Revolution had no value whatsoever. In terms of industrialism, women went from having few rites to having equal writes. During the seventeenth and eighteenth century, women were just coming on the job seen. It wasn't until 1830 with the passing of the child labor laws that women started to show up in the textile factories, mills, and mines. The revolution invented new clothes so women no longer had to wear their old garbage.

In 1842 the legislature decided to end women's work in the mines and the reason was because they couldn't envision women working topless. Other women were continually sexually harassed by overseers. They were fined for talking or being late to work. Women of this time went through hell and decided to put their foot down. During the early nineteenth century, women were excluded from the work place by working class organizations who forced the ideology of domesticity. This meant that women should not work, but should stay home to bare and nurture children.

The working class women who didn't get jobs turned to prostitution, not because it was fun, but as a way to survive. Also, the changes to wage earners gave lots of men and women time to flirt. This created illegitimate children. Children were becoming people and they evoked concern, especially in the work force. Long hours and very little education meant that factory children would grow up to be nobodies.

Factory working conditions were very bad. Children worked in places that were like sweet boxes; this created sickness. Most children died in the factories and work areas of industrialization. Working conditions in the factories also provided diseases like syndrome in younger males due to malnutrition.[160] In 1821, coal mines used children to haul the carts up to the lifts. With the heat unbearable and crawl spaces only about eight inches high, many came out with deformed bodies and damaged lungs.

Over all, the Industrial Revolution really took the traditional roles of women and children and swung them around. Kids weren't kids and families had to find new ways to support themselves. Many were looking for balance and an answer.

The Industrial Revolution was not one of blood, sweat, and tears, however, but rather one of coal, oil, and machinery. The inventions really hit it off well. There were many outbreakings of machines.[161] Britain produced a lot of profit from the college industry, which gave it a large supply of capital for investment in new machines. John Kay developed the power veneer and the Fly and Shuttle which doubled the output of cotton in the 1730s. Now the spinners couldn't keep up with the weavers, which created a bottleneck need for more string to be created.

---

[160] While young male workers got syndromes, young females usually got complexes, and children suffered stomach aches from licking too many sweet boxes.

[161] Between 1810 and 1820, the radical Luddites were especially good at "outbreaking of machines."

But James Hargreaves improved the flying shuttle in the 1760s and helped out in this bottleneck. Herrigan invented the spinning jenny and named it after John Regreves' wife, Jenny.[162] In 1769 a very important invention, the water power wheel, was dreamed up. Then in 1779, Richard Achrite invented the water frame, water wheel, water mule, and water-powered spinner, which was big and expensive. In the same year, Samuel Crompton took the spinning jenny and water frame and put them together and called it a hybrid spinning mule.

Britain produced a lot of profit from the college industry

David Arkwright created water and animals that powered water into frame spinning machines. Richard Cartwright then invented the water fence and the power loon in 1785 that allowed the merchantization of textiles to be removed from the home and into the factory. Robert Blakewell invented the time clock used in factories. The inventions such as the flying shuttle, the spinning jenny, and steam power provided the artillery for this revolution.

Coke was converted into pig iron or steel by means of an open hearth or pudding method invented by Thomas Darby. Collies replaced charcoal in the iron and steel productions.[163] Because of the abundance of coal and

---

[162] Regreves was Herrigan's cousin, twice removed, and his wife Jenny could spin like a top on the dance floor.

[163] The Royal Society for the Prevention of Cruelty to Animals, however, soon stopped the use of collies for fuel.

iron, this caused cities to uproot. With the coming of industrialization came urbanization, with European cities growing population wise, industrial wise, and political wise.

The cities became overwhelmingly crowded. Everyone wanted to come to Europe for a new beginning and the cities weren't ready. Overcrowding meant that people lived on top of each other. The poor people had to live in slums which were filled with filth and diseases such as chlorea.[164] Cars were another reason that industrialization from 1830 to 1850 hurt Europe.

Due to the lack of municipal direction, open sewers and drains were common along the streets. The sewers were inadequate, so human waste was simply thrown into the street or rivers, making fishing undesirable. In fact, the stench of the cities and towns was so horrible that they could be smelled from miles away. As one walked down the street, human and animal feces were everywhere. The germs were bred there and their life was very, very dirty. Everything stunk.

Lack of sanitation and cleanliness caused diseases and a terrible outbreak of cholrea. The smell of death reeked in the air. It was estimated that death rates outnumbered birth rates. So the Albert Embankment sewer system was built along the Thames River in France.

Social and economic expectations placed on the lower classes made others mad and they committed a lot of arson on property. One group, the Chartists, had six demands in a petition they presented: all male sufferage, the secret ballad, abolition of MPs property, equal electoral districts, payment for members of Parliament, and a forgotten sixth one.

There was a need for a policed society. They kept cities in order and helped maintain crime against property.[165] Many felt that the increase of crime was because of social deprivation, social expectations, or the existence of a criminal sect. The establishment of new scientifically designed prisons (called hulks) was spurred by great people like John Howard, Eliza Frey, and "Hulk" Hogan.

The prison reform created terrible conditions in state prisons such as the Bastille, local prisons, and the authoritarian system. The police were created to look after domestic duties. Even Pope Leo IV organized the Paris police force. In France, the police grew from 500 to 4000. They

---

[164] Chlorea was on the rise as people in the slums were drinking more chlorinated water now.

[165] In some areas, to keep policemen from being laid off, law enforcement charities encouraged the criminal element to maintain a minimum level of property crimes.

were called *gendermere*. These different groups of police helped maintain odor, protect property, and incest crimes. Crime was prevented just at the sign of a police officer.

Another method of punishment was the transportation of criminals out of the country to colonies like New Wales, Australia, which was previously Georgia in the USA. In America, the Auburn prison system separated prisoners only at night. The Philadelphia system emphasized constant separation, which led to metal breakdowns.[166]

Chartist demands included the secret ballad

Nineteenth-century nationalists didn't care about individual freedom; they shot down liberalism. But the idea of equality under the law and liberalism was supported by Thomas Malthus and the likes of Metternich and Nicholas I (also known as the policeman of Europe), who were leaders in the Quadruple Alliance that was pro-nationalism and pro-liberalism.

Metternich was a paranoid man and was constantly looking out for evidence of liberalism and nationalism. Most of the revolts from 1820 to 1848 were put down. Usually another country came in and shut them down. In the 1820s the countries of Spain, France, Italy, Britain, Latin America, and Greece experienced revolutions of one kind or another.

In Spain, the army, upper middle class merchants, and liberal intellectuals revolted in 1820. This revolt was crushed, however, when

---

[166] Unable to hack this isolation, inmates sawed their way through the metal bars of their cells.

Nicholas I intervened and restored Ferdinand to the throne. Then Ferdinand destroyed the cortes, an elected Parliament assembly, and all its members. In Russia, the secret societies revolted against Alex X because of strict and arbitrary censorship.

In Belgium in 1820, the people were against their Turkish masters. The students revolted and this spread throughout Belgium. Because the revolts violated the Venice Arrangement of 1815, Austria, Prussia, and Russia wanted to help, but France and Great Britain said no.

Some revolutionary fervor even spilled out of Europe into Latin America, where Spain still held colonies until the mid-1830s. Napoleon's manhandling of Spain had weakened its grip on the colonies and when they got a whiff of liberalism, they ran with it. The armies also revolted and there were several wins.

In the 1830s, the countries of Italy, France, Britain, Spain, Russia, Belgium, and Austria experienced revolutions. Hungary became independent within Russia. The French were bickering over who was to be the air of the throne.

Africa and Asia were divided up between these European nations. It was the white man's burden to civilize the savages and they attacked it with gusto.[167]

In 1848 all states had liberal constitutions except Lombardy and Venetia. France in 1848 set up a republic with universal male suffrage. Women began protesting in Lyon, the silk-weaving place, but no one knows why. Probably long hours and low wages.

Hearing of the revolution of 1848 in Paris, craftsmen and workers in Germany went wild with joy and intellectuals were set on fire.

---

[167] In many places where these Europeans set foot, they first fell on their knees and then upon the aborigines, attacking them with gusto as well.

19

Romantics Were the New Agers of Their Day

Romanticism was a more liberal, romantic, open type of thinking. I'm OK, you're OK, the whole world is OK basically. The Romanticist believed one should have that self-belief in oneself. Romanticism badly clashed with the ideals and fundamentals of the Conservatives. Romanticism was about change and freedom. Conservatism avoided change like the Bubonic Plague. Therefore, Romanticism and Conservatism are almost anonyms. Their ideals were based on too different an idea. Romanticism was "free-falling," more liberal, and embraced change.

The closeness to the earth was very important to the Romantic period. People built their houses surrounded by forests so they could walk in them and let their Romantic feelings out. They had very loud and upbeat music compared to the Enlightenment; it is fondly referred to today as the "long-haired music."

The Dark Ages fascinated the Romanticists partly because this was the age of no reason when barbarism was in. Romantic writers believed in human nature, against what Enlightenment writers found to be human nature of rationality. The Romantics studied history, religion, and folk traditions. They were the New Agers of their day. Romantics such as Lord Byron and William Woodsworth could write and paint about such beauty as God created. Tennyson wrote a poem called "Grave's Energy."[168]

Romantics were critical of growing industrialization. They felt it squelched man's knowledge and acceptance of the simple life. Some of

---

[168] This poem, which resembled an elegy, was written in a cemetery, so it was very grave indeed.

the Romantics practiced bizarre behavior, such as one woman who stabbed herself to make herself a better poet.[169]

The Dark Ages fascinated the Romanticists because this was the age of no reason when barbarism was in

The religious sector had a rough time during the nineteenth century. There was a clash between church and state. Many people left the church because it was organized. But the Catholics and Protestants always seemed to pull through. The Catholic Church had a seductive mystery to it. A church council met and declared the pope infallible, almost immortal.[170] Then one priest wanted a monarchy so he elected Pope Pious IX to the throne.

In England, being a minority, the Utilitarians didn't like the idea of most of the teachers being Angelicans. John Stuart Mill believed in the right of every man to swing his fist, but not the right to punch someone's face. Malphis believed in all these preventions of population growth

---

[169] She got the point and her poetry sharply improved, although she died soon afterwards.

[170] Church councils had often declared previous popes immoral, but this was the closest any pope ever came to immortality.

because he believed God saw them to be OK and one doesn't argue with a minister. His theory of the "iron law of wages" stated that an organization can profit in the long run by paying the worker the least possible amount necessary for him to live.

Art became a subject of study. One had to study some paintings to make any sense out of them. There were no clear-cut lines such as one fills in when coloring in a coloring book. Paintings moved away from showing stuck-up rich snobs.

The use of the paint brush was one of the changes. Most of all, a change was seen from the fine-line stroke to the fat, flat blob. Van Gough, for example, was somewhat riotous in his colors. The painters were so natural as to paint a nudist. They painted more realistic pictures, such as farms and the nice girl next door nude on a picnic with four other men. This portrays Naturalism—it is so natural because she forgot her clothes.

From the mid-nineteenth century, Europeans were reading more. By 1860, more people were catching on to literacy. The attack on illeturacy was successful in Britain, France, Belgium, The Neverlands, Germany, and Scandanify. In 1868 Hungary took part in learning how to read. In 1870 Britain and in 1874 Switzerland became literate.

Emilie Zola turned realism into a movement. She wrote *Nana* in 1880.[171] Zola hated details of crimes and political scandals because she thought it should be written the way it really was. The Realist writers wrote about the realism of life the way it really was. It did not portray a pretty colored picture. They wrote about how people are—animalistic—and how life is. In Britain, for example, prostitution became legal. Realists took away the colored picture and produced the gray pictures of life then.[172]

Other Realist writers were Gustave Flombert, Ivan Tergenor, and Emile Zora. Zora went on to write the *Germinal* novel about French mine conditions along with Jeanne Bouvier who was an active feminist and an organizer fighting for women's rights. Samuel Richardson, a British author, helped women gain stature through the novel. His works *Pamela* in 1940 and *Clarissa* in 1948 were influential in establishing women's roles. Henrik Endsen wrote "The Doll's House" about a woman who finally walked out on her husband.

---

[171] This less well-known sister of the famous French novelist deserves much more attention than historians have generally accorded her in the past.

[172] The smoke, ash, and pollution of the Industrial Revolution had befogged the air over Europe, ruining many a good color painting during this era.

20

Evolution Presents a Mixed Bog of Truth and Error

Science was introduced by an Englishman, Charles Darwin, who was the inventor of Darwinism. Now more people knew what science was.

Karl Marx and Charles Darwin applied evolution to society in their books. Darwin's book *The Decent of Man* was published ten years after Karl Marx's book *The Origin of Species*. Darwin gained much of his theory from a minister named Thomas Malphis. In 1854 Darwin published *Origin of Man*, which took Evolution beyond physical nature and applied it to living beings, yet not humans. He stressed the similarities between man and beast in his book *Nature of Tooth and Claw*.

In Darwinism, only the fittest survive and the fittest mate with other fittest, creating the fittest offspring. Due to variations, some organisms were naturally selected to survive. Those naturally selected to survive, survived. This led to the survival of the fittest.

In economics, survival of the fittest came into play. Businesses said that the best would survive and the weak guy would get kicked out. They used this as an excuse to knock out the little guy. John D. Rockefeller stated that in order for the biggest success to be achieved, all the other little people must be trimmed off the rose bush of life so that the biggest rose could be produced. Of course, that rose had to be a Rockefeller. Survival of the fittest meant that you should do unto others before they do unto you.[173]

---

[173] This inverted version of the Golden Rule is commonly known as the Iron Rule of Nature.

But Evolution presents a mixed bog of truth and error in its aspects of micro- versus macro-evolution, the time span, its rejection of a Savior, and through proofs accurately portraying organic evolution. Darwinism totally did away with the creationistic view. For example, if the Garden of Eden didn't exist, then the origin of sin is erased because an amoeba can't sin. It's kind of hard for a one-celled amoeba to eat the forbidden fruit.

Darwinism thus caused people to question their own existence. Previously people believed that they were unique and designed by God. But now these people were instilled with fear and anxiety about the possibility of breeding finer humans.

Charles Darwin changed the thinking of all of Europe, threatened a steadfast religion, changed politics, and may have even caused World War I.[174] From his theories came the concept of the supper race.

Sociology changed because racial prejudice was introduced. Darwinism caused such a change in the thinking of the world that it might have been better off had he gotten stranded forever on the Galapagos Islands.

From Darwin's theories came the concept of the supper race

---

[174] Most monographs on the evolution of the Great War overlook this causative possiblity.

21

Otto von Bismarck
Screwed Up the World

Germany was not unified before 1870 due to the lack of unity. It also took so long to become unified because of disunity. While Germany did not yet exist, however, there were many little providences. Yet finally, unification loomed over the horizon as a big ball of possibility.

German unification was led by the Persian government under the rule of William I. By 1830 all German states except Austria were united under the Prussian Parliament. Two groups stood out in the Frankfurt Assembly. The *grossdeutch*, which wanted to include Austria in the unification, and the *driseldeutch*, which wanted a smaller Germany. King William the Forth bestowed upon Otto von Brunswick the title of Chancellor. Then when he died in 1859, William the First was crowned King of Prussia.

Otto von Bismarck was chancellor of Germany and Prussia and prime minister of Austria. He was a shrew politician and military leader. He became prime minister of Germany in 1862 and gave his "Blood and Iron" inaugural address. He was known as blood and guts.

Bismarck and William I also built a very strong army which he called the Junckers.[175] Vell, Bismarck wanted to test his army, so he brought on wars. The needle gun aided greatly the success of Prussia's defeat of Denmark as a goad to force Austria into war. The Austrian-Prussian War,

---

[175] This army of Junckers and a strong navy of Jalopies made a formidable force with which to screw up the world.

the French War, and the war with the Spaniards were three wars Bismarck led Germany into.

The French got so upset when the Spanish throne was offered to Leopold, a relative of William I, because this would mean that they would be surrounded by the Hollenzein. At the end of the Franco-Prussian War, Germany got greedy and annexiated Alsace-Lorraine. In the Danish War of 1864, Denmark wanted Schleswig and Holstein, but the Prussians declared war on the Danes and won. Bismarck then split Alsace and Lorraine with Austria.

This war laid the foundation for the Austral-Prussian War which came in 1866 following tension between Austria and Prussia. Prussia did not take away any land, but persuaded Austria to annex Schleswig and Holstein and a number of other small states, which Prussia turned into the Confederation of North German States, excluding Austria.

The Prussian armies with Otto had many successful revolutions to unify Germany. He was the unfortunate leader of Germany then who screwed up the world. Then on January 18, 1871, at the Hall of Mirrors in Versailles, King William I was named kaiser of the Second German Republic. Then Otto von Bismarck replaced Napoleon III and formed a new republic. A national assembly was formed and was working until March 26, when the republic set up an independent republic called the Commune.

Italy took so long to become unified because of its divided nature. It was divided into many different parts with different control by France and Russia. Italy was expansionistic, changing ports from the Mediterranean to the Atlantic. Also, regionalism between the different providences discouraged its unification.

The Risorgimento movement was a free vote to see who was and was not interested in unifying Italy. The Kingdom of the Two Cities was then defeated and taken by Italy.

Gamibaldi, a rebel who used his men trained with gorilla tactics in the struggles of 1848-49, went next and fought the two Sicilies and won with fewer than twenty times the Redcoats that they had. Manzini founded the Young Turks and both he and Garabelli were Romantic Republican Nationalists.[176] Because of Manzini's tactics of throwing people against people, this is the reason it took such a long period of time

---

[176] In this wildly Romantic era, heroes like Princip, Gamibaldi, Manzini, and Garabelli served the revolutionary needs of Italians, Turks, and Sicilians with equal fervor.

before Italy became a nation-state. Manzini led a movement called the ricegimento which sought to reform Italy into a republic.[177]

Gorilla tactics

Then a club of women called the Carbonari, along with the National Guard, armed themselves and forced King Gerbennad the First to return to Paris and grant a constitution and a Parliamentary government. Italy was having the same problem with Louis Philippe during the revolts. So King Victor Emmanuel II was responsible for getting Napoleon II to sign the Bourdiar Agreement, which meant that should Austria invade Italy, then France would help out.

Cavour, a conservative liberalist and architect of Italy, felt that Austria must be kicked out of Piedmont and Vienna. Using his wit, he

---

[177] Japan contributed significantly to this ricegimento movement in Italy by sending coolies to help plant rice paddies next to the pimento fields.

convinced France to aid them in their struggle. Piedmont, as well as the rest of Italy, needed canons and training in order to fight Austria. Nicholas III, King of France, agreed to such terms as long as they agreed with the public opinion of France and Europe. In return, Nicholas III's cousin, Prince Nicholas, would be marrying Victor Emmanuel's younger daughter.[178] So in 1848 France became a nation.

Italy and other Latin American countries also experienced liberal constitutions. The Austrian armies tried to force a liberalist constitution on the Italian people. By the Treaty of Villafranca with Austria, Italy received Lombardy but not Spain.

Finally, Italy crushed Austria at Magneta de Solfernio, and Austria signed the Treaty of Prague. The influence of the wars caused Tuscany, Parma, Romagna, and Modena to revolt. These, with the other German states, formed the Northern German Confederation.

The Prussians indirectly helped finish the unification of Italy by withdrawing their troops during the Franco-Prussian War. Unification was complete by 1972 when Prince William of Piedmont became the new king and Emmanuel II said, "Italy is made." It was a long process, but finally it was a realization to the talented, emotional, fiery Italians.

Cavour helped unify Italy in the Hall of Mirrors in Versailles, then died six months later. But after Rome became the capital of Italy, the country became a hole. So Keir Hardie chose Cavour to be Prime Minister of England.[179]

---

[178] Her name was Victoria Emmanuella.

[179] Like the revolutionaries mentioned in footnote 176, prime ministers were equally willing to serve in whatever countries had a need for their services. The Prime Ministers' Club sent out periodic notices of job openings across Europe.

22

The Wife of a Prime Minister Is a Primate

Ever since the beginning of time, men have held dominion over women. Their gender shows whether such a man is masculine, feminine, or neuter. Thousands of years of oppression ain't going to change overnight.

Women were the weaker sex and were most often expected to be ladies, not Amazons. In the 1870s, women were treated as less than equals, for they were considered to be less than human. Even Queen Victoria caused male opposition in England toward suffrage to harden. She was the first to oppose the movement, calling it the "bloody suffrage movement," this "mad, wild thing," and "the mad bother of wickedness." Primer Minister Stuart Asqueth was very much against women's rights.

In the early eighteenth century during World War I, women had no property or voting rights. But suffrage was the in thing. Britain gave women the right to vote in 1780 in local elections, for England was the first to let women work, while Germany at this time gave women no rights. The Flapper Bill gave women of 21 the same voting rights of men in 1814.

The women's movement was divided between suffragettes and suffrages. Marry Wollenslung, author of *Victory of the Right of Woman*, was the first known feminist.

Disraeli wrote an "Essay on the Subjection of Women" to enlighten men and women what their needs and wants might be. Melinda Fawcett thought that Parliament would listen to women if they could prove themselves. Keir Hardie introduced the Independence Labor Party for women and proworkers.

John Mill was a great philosophical thinker, utilitarian, radical member of the House of Commerce, and a helper of the sufferages. His concept was subjection of women in 1869. He wanted to insert "mankind" in the bill to make it applicable to women in 1867. He was also supported by Benjamin Diarson. Mill's attempts to put in for women to be able to vote didn't work and it was out the door.

Things were not looking good, and the women were starting to get radical about this. In the years leading up to 1914, women were becoming more alive and an outspoken part of society. Emily Bankhurt and her daughters Silvia and Christilia were leaders of the radical movement. The Ladies National Association, or LNA, was led by Emily Dankhert and brought unity to women.[180] Women such as Olympe de Gouges, Marie Condorcet, and Mary Wollstonecraft, proved instrumental and helpful in getting women's views across to others and also in spreading the liberal feeling to other females. Women set up saloons where they could hold meetings with men and talk politics.

Women set up saloons where they could hold meetings with men and talk politics

---

[180] Most of those in the inner circle of suffragette leadership, it seems, were named Emily.

Mary Drummond and Mrs. Buntop introduced the hunger strike on July 1, 1910, for three to four days while in prison. Prime Minister Aquist made a rule against releasing women who went on hunger strikes. It said that when they were better, they were put back in jail. The worst incident against suffragettes was "Black Friday," when the policemen trying to control a women's protest march lost their tempers and started violently hitting, kicking, and beating the demonstrators. This was the "Black War." Women for suffrage had to be willing to suffer for their rights, sometimes by violent means, such as riots, resisting arrest, kicking, and screaming.

The men in their ignorance thought that if women had the right to vote they wouldn't be able to bare children anymore. One of the four barbarisms against women in England was that they did not have the right to have children in a dispute with a husband.

There were, however, many women who fought against their poor treatment, women such as Emily Pankhurst and her two daughters who were suffergettes. They started doing wild things to be noticed by government politicians and the press. Mrs. Pankhurst founded the Women's Social Policies Union and the National American Suffrage Association.[181] She used violent tactics for women's rights in group demonstrations led by suffragates (a bishop without a diocese is a suffragate, whereas the wife of a prime minister is a primate). These women painted King Edward's box in suffragette colors of purple, white, and green, and burned his lawn with acid.

Emily Dickinson became a martyr for the cause of women's suffrage when she threw herself in front of the emperor's carriage at the Epson Derby horse race.[182] At her funeral, thousands of women attended wearing purple, white, and yellow. Then Edward VIII was in favor of women's votes.

Women suffragettes also refused jailment when possible. On September 17, 1909, women were forced to eat by putting hoses in their noses.[183] They were force-fed by the tube, gag, and drool method. Then the Cat and Mouse Act said that when a woman went on a hunger strike while in jail, she would be sent home, fattened up, and put back in jail, which definitely put a strain on a household.

---

[181] Like Italian revolutionaries and prime ministers, these long-suffering British suffragettes eagerly served the needs of whatever country desired them.

[182] As the crowd surrounded her on the racetrack, her famous last words were, "I'm nobody, who are you?"

[183] This was the beginning of the liquid diet craze in Britain.

David Lloyd George stated, "Either let women vote or kill them." Winston Churchill and Edward Grey were liberal leaders of suffrage. Eventually John Stuart Mill did get a clause put into the Voting Rights Act to give British women the right to vote at 30 in 1918 when World War I broke out. Women's roles in helping men in World War II thus earned them the right to vote. So Joseph Mills and Disraeli tried to get the Reform Act to include women as mankind.

Meanwhile in the United States, Congress said women were only three things: angels, helpmeats, and inferriers.[184]

During the 1920s, the length of a woman's dress rose and they started to get in touch with and gain control over their sexuality. Women got positive gains in that they had a right to sexual satisfaction. They had the right to orgasms. Women were endowed with good sanitation and an ample amount of electricity. It was the age of the Flapper; thin was in, like Twiggy. Women were becoming feminine, elegant, and serene.

Women were becoming feminine, elegant, and serene

In family and home life, women gained a more independent role than before. Women weren't pulling out babies left and right, so their attention was placed more diligently on their new children. Birth rates

---

[184] In short, feathers, flesh, and iron oxide rather than sugar, spice, and everything nice.

dropped because of the use of birth control and condoms. More infants were surviving their early childhood days. Therefore, the sheer progeny of childbirth caused the decline of pregnancies.

Since most middle class families could not afford servants, these women worked extra hard to maintain the appearance of idleness. By World War I, this new portrayal of women was spurred on by the silent movies and much later, of course, by TV. Marilyn Monroe was a good example: how many times did one see her in a kitchen baking pies and wiping kids' runny noses?

Women started to make movements in Europe and the United States. Though she failed, Elizabeth Blackwell was accepted at the Geneva School of Medicine by mistake. Doors of opportunity for women opened further for those who followed Florence Nightingale, a participant in the American Civil War, and Clare Bonton, a nurse in the Crimean War.[185] Women were peace workers, but they were overworked and especially overpaid.

In France, there was an abundance of farms and here one could see women cultivating, weaving, spinning, and picking cotton in the fields and workforce. As bigger, better, faster machines were invented, employment underwent a shift. The mind-numbing, high-speed jobs basically had women written all over them, and yet men complained that women were stealing their jobs.

In pre-World War II society, the family had meals together and mom's main function was to bare children. Women did, however, receive some serious losses. Because of the advancing technology of this time, many women were being put out of jobs. The cotton ginny put many women out of work along with the development of other farm equipment. Female prostitutes were usually unskilled and poor. They were often slaves or orphans and remained prostitutes for only a few years and then either re-entered the work force or married.

---

[185] Once again, like Italian revolutionaries and British suffragettes, nurses in those days were "citizens of the world," ready to serve whatever country offered them a nice, bloody war in which to practice their art.

23

Carol Marx Began Marxism

Utopian and Marxist Socialism differ as a dream world differs from the scientific world. The trampling of the urban working class and the apparent callousness of their task masters inspired various socialist groups. The responses of two of these, the Luddites and the Sabots, can be mildly understood because they felt that their lives were being taken from them.[186] After all, their abilities and skills were being replaced by machinery. They must have cared about their society in order to take a stand as they did, even though it involved destruction.

First of all, Utopian Socialism was very different, very idealistic, very dream-landish. It offered only cosmetic improvements to society. Utopian Charles Fourier tried his hand at Utopian Socialism by setting up phalanxes. Women could not work independently because of low wages, so they took up the family life. Their goal was to have kids and care for them.

Robert Owen had a factory in Scotland called New Landmark. There, this British industrialist was appalled by the conditions at the cotton mills of New Landmark, so he gave the workers better homes, more pay, and shortened hours.[187] Thus, he increased in productivity and profit, while the workers had higher morals. This was the first factory to run smoothly.

---

[186] While the Luddites of England destroyed machinery with sledgehammers, the Sabots of France used their wooden shoes, or sabots, to jam belts and gears, giving rise to the terms "saboteurs" and "sabotage."

[187] Josiah Wedgewood's new factory clock could be wound to run fast, thus cutting three to five minutes off each hour. Factory hands loved these time clocks and quickly adapted to them at New Landmark.

In England, the Fabian Society's main members were Sidney and Beatrice Wells and George B. Shaw. Over in Germany, the German socialist Hegel had his theory of Hegelism. It was this dialect that Marx borrowed in which all things evolve and all change in time through antagonism between one thing to another. Hegel was more of a Spiritualist while Marx focused on material needs.

Unlike Utopianism, Marxism wanted a total change in the world, not just minor reforms. Carol Marx, along with the son of a wealthy industrialist, Fred Engels, began Marxism. Carol Marx was no relation to Groucho.[188]

Marx was from Germany, Western Germany, to be exact. His career was in journalism, which explains a little why he was so inquisitive. Marx went to work at his father's factory in England. Then he started the Communist Manirecto with Angles, which taught the Helentism Dialectic.

Marx believed that the working class of proletariat would overpower and intermesh with the middle class to form one big happy family. He said one has to take the slum out of the man before one can take the man out of the slum. He based his theory that the proletariat would one day kill the bourgeoisie in a violent revolution on Machiavelli's theory that the end justifies the means. One example of this theory applied in France was when the French National Assembly disbanded the Commune in May 1871 and in the process killed 20,000 people. This caused tension.

This caused tension

---

[188] Carol, Karl Marx's second wife, exerted much more influence in establishing socialist ideals than she is given credit for. Her relationship with Fred Engels deserves further study.

ℰᏜ   Ꮬℛ

Marxism had some ideas that were controversial. One was that man is the supreme being over god. There was the dialectic theory that everything evolves. The classes would change and go to whatever, without influence or political interference. This caused serious problems because no one wanted to believe that things would take care of themselves. No one studied to be the best either, so society ratings fell.

Marxists wanted a classless society now and full of blood.[189] Marx published *The Communist Manifesto* in 1848 with Frederick Hegel and *Das Kapital* in 1917, which advocated a classless society. Despite Karl Marx never having or getting a haircut, a lot of people followed him.

Marxism was impractical, however, because it didn't supply enough religious and individualism fuel to keep his followers burning. But studying history sure makes one struggle, so maybe Marx had a point.

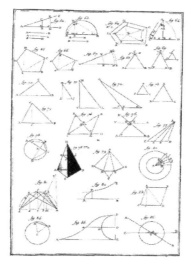

Marx started the Communist Manirecto with Angles

---

[189] To its credit, Marxism over the past century has provided its adherents with plenty of opportunities for full-blooded social interaction in riots, revolts, and revolutions of all kinds.

24

Hitler Killed the Jews
With Firing Squid

Gavrillo Princip, the commander of the ship *Panther* (which was parked outside Adgavir), later became a patriarch of the Serbian Orthodox Church in Yugoslavia and influenced his country's support of the Allies in World War II.[190] Austrian Archduke Francis Ferdinand and his wife were killed in Barsnia by the Black Hand terrorist Gernio Princip.[191]

In Europe, there was political unrest in the tinder box, which were the small countries that made up central Europe like Serbia, Latvia, Turkey and Bulgaria. International rivalry was growing by leaps and bounds. As less space was available for more growth, countries were running into each other.[192]

From 1848 to 1914, a united Germany was the single most important European country. By 1914, Britain, France, Germany, Portugal, Spain, Belgium, and Russia had carved up Africa among themselves, leaving only Liberia and Ethiopia independent. Russia acquired Alaska and began to settle Siberia. By 1914, 90% of Siberians were slaves.

Nations got involved in war because a duke was killed. The assassination of Francis Ferdinand and his wife on June 28, 1914, was the feather that broke the camel's back.

---

[190] Princip's secret society, the Black Hand, recruited Mensa-quality individuals who were equally adept at throwing bombs, commanding ships, fathering churches, and conducting bellicose diplomacy.

[191] Gernio, a saboteur or wooden shoe maker, was the first cousin of Gavrillo Princip; he sometimes earned extra pocket money as a hired assassin.

[192] This collision of countries was also due to the aftershocks of continental drift.

By 1914, Austria hated the Serbs, Russia hated the Germans, and France seriously disliked the Germans. Now the respective lines were drawn, so all that was needed was a spark to light the gas-soaked wool in the Balkans.

The Triple Entente was made up of France, Germany and Russia, while the Triple Alliance, started at the Congress of Berlin in 1798, was made up of Germany, Italy, and Austria-Hungary. When the Russians left Germany and joined France and England, this created more bad blood with Germany.

Alliances were very flakey in that nations joined more than one over conflicts of interest. They took most of what the Belgarians had gained since 1878. The Belgarians felt that France did not oppose the German invasion, except through their Magnet Line of defense. Meanwhile, Britain established a protectorate over Egypt. They advanced into the Sedans.[193]

Compared to World War II, World War I, the War to End All Wars, looked almost like a playground tussle. But it was no picnic.

World War I looked almost like a playground tussle

---

[193] WWI witnessed many innovations. The French Magnet Line used a powerful electromagnetic field to hold any advancing tanks and armored vehicles stationary until destroyed. The British conquered Egypt due to their advantage in using the new four-door double-armored tanks called sedans.

The war began in 1918 and lasted for four years. There was virtually no movement in those four years. Dogfights were also a new part of the war, while U-boats or submarines were new ways to bomb ships. William II of Germany began building ships and more warships to have a powerful sea army. Submarines were forced to surface every half hour to recharge their batteries; this made them susceptible to trash cans.[194]

Offensive attacks consisted of heavy artillery barrages used offensively to soften up enemy lines. Then followed a great charge of men with buoynets.

A great charge of men with buoynets

The carrier sea ships were created to carry fighter planes. The British had new tanks (the Sedans), new underground trenches, and bob wire. Trench warfare baffled generals used to movement. Living in a trench, however, meant that one had to live with the ones that weren't.

---

[194] Primarily because passing battleships and cruisers could not see the darkened hulls of the U-boats at night when they threw their garbage pails overboard. Hitting the hull of a submarine with a 50-gallon trash can could impair the hearing of crew members inside. It gave rise to the expression "We've been canned."

Russia withdrew from the war and signed the Treaty of Breast-Litovos with Germany in case of a German victory. To get back at France and Russia, Germany called for a conference in Algiers, Spain, to discuss France's control of Morocco. Germany wanted Morocco, but Spain got it. Germany got nothing.

In 1917, World War I ended when France wanted reparations money because they had had to pay Germany money in the Napoleonic War. It is evident that World War I caused many wounds to be healed.

Germany after the war could only have six battle ships. They couldn't weigh over 10,000 pounds apiece.[195] In the 1920s, Germany was in a shambles, physically and economically. The German mark was worth the paper it was printed on.

The British were worried because of the commercial and navel competition that the United States was doing against the French.[196] Georges Clemenceau also wanted France to pay monetarily for the atrocities of World War I.

The 1920s roared in with new happenings. This is when they voted Warren B. Harrison into the presidency.[197] People were drinking more than ever, especially since it was illegal.

Then during the 1930s Depression, a worldwide epidemic, agrigoods turned down in price and tariffs went up. There was a cod slump due to the use of hydroelectric factories.[198]

Democratic European governments didn't let the Depression be an economic one for them. United States President Harry S. Truman announced a one-year moratorium on all international debts in 1932. Over in Britain, the "Land Girls" manned—or womanned—the fields, plowing, planting, and harvesting.

In Germany, the Nazis, known as the National Socialists Party, were happy. They had found their leader. He was a dream come true.

---

[195] The recent invention of plastics made these light-weight battleships possible.

[196] These navel contests of the '20s soon led to full-fledged beauty contests, resulting in the Miss Universe Pageant which began in 1929.

[197] Warren B. Harrison was the great-grandson of former president William H. Harrison and second cousin of the next president Warren G. Harding, who came to office when Harrison died of eating too many frozen cherries on a hot July day.

[198] Cod and other fish kept getting caught in the intake valves of these hydro-electric plants, whose huge fans chopped them into tiny bits. Eventually this led to a booming business in cod liver oil.

A song sung by the German people sums it up: "There is no freedom for one unless there is freedom for all." Adolf Hitler was an Austrian-born German immigrant who believed in an Aryan ideal and German dominance. His mother was very religious and to Adolf, she was a perfect angle which he worshipped and adored. Later in life Hitler enjoyed the religious exercises at the local monastery and thought about entering it so he could become an abbot (he didn't think much of the Costello type).

He was not the most intelligent man, but he had an air of authority. He was authoritarian and totalitarian. Little did men know that he was not one who would allow himself to be walked on. Hitler was quite sly.

It was said that Hitler aroused more on the radio than he did in person. He made use of mass media techniques through posters, newspapers, textbooks, magazines, radio, motion pictures, television, telephones, and teletypes. Propaganda and media control was headed by Josef Gobbler.[199]

Propaganda was headed by Josef Gobbler

In his two books, *Mein Comphe* and *Mie Kumf*, Hitler laid out his plans long in advance and was ready when President Hindenburg died to take charge by combining the positions of president and chancellor and

---

[199] Appropriately, Gobbler had been a former poultry farmer, but he made the adjustment from propagating turkeys to propagating lies quite smoothly.

calling himself "Furher dur Kariter."[200] He had an obsession with power. He wanted to have a total following and thus he created a mass hallucination. As he would drive by, the people would raise their arms and shout, "Heil, Hitler!" He gained the confidence of Germany's conquerors and received permission to re-arm Germany. He formed the Brown Uniforms, originated a new salute ("High Hitler!"), new emblems and flags (the shticke).

The Nazis had many different police forces—the S.A., the S.S., and the Govorras. Hitler was after *lemberium*, elbow room, and *lebrunism*, or living space, to support his master race. In his next book, *My Kemph*, Hitler said that he was looking to Russia and her vassal states to provide this *lebrunism*. The Allies didn't realize that he was a very pieceful man: he wanted a piece of all the European nations.

Germany wanted a world empire called the Third Rhic. Neither Britain nor France wanted to engage in another war since they had both lost in World War I. Hitler also spent money on a new air force, the Lufftan.[201]

Then the Nazis turned to the terrible means of gas chambers, concentration camps, and much worse violence. They used a secret police called The Troops. Reinhark Heinrich, the leader of the S.S. (Secrudy Service), was given the task of rounding up all the Jews after the defeat in Poland and placing them in the ghettos throughout the Polish cities. At first, though, Hitler shipped Jews to Madagascar.

Later, the extermination of the Jews was administered by Heinrich Herdrich, head of the Secret Service, and Himmler, one of Mussolini's devoted followers. They assembled the S.S., an intensive, sadistic set of men who carried out their orders to the limit. Herdrich and Himmler headed up what was called the final solution. The Nazis killed six to eight million Jews using concentration camps, torture, gas chambers, and firing squid.[202]

The Nazi government by 1943 had started removing women and children from urban areas to rural areas. This was hard on the urbanites because the rural people were mean to them.

The Jews were taken to death camps and concentration camps and made to be less than even a cat or dog. There were six main concentration camps; the largest was at Auschen-Britenav. During World War

---

[200] Or in English, "Leader with Character." Events soon proved that he was indeed a character!

[201] Lufftan means "tanned wing," implying that its pilots, who were exposed to the sun for long periods to toughen them up, were well tanned.

[202] The Nazis discovered that the jet-black ink of the squid was a potent poison when shot from high-powered water guns.

II, the most devastating aspect of the war was this systematic elimination of human life by the Germans. This was the cause of never-before-seen amounts of lost life.

Hitler signed with Mussolini a steel pact that if either were to become involved in a war, they would aid each other. In 1936, Japan and Germany made the Anti-Contitern Pact. Hitler threatened the Austrians with invasion and forced the Austrian chancellor, Kurt von Schnigg, to put Austrian Nazis in power. He then took Austria and asked for Serbia.

Despite the Serbians' great desire for independence, Neville Chamberblow of Britain (1869-1970) agreed to let Germany take Serbia and siege Chicovolk in an attempt to avoid war. On March 13, 1938, Hitler annexed Austria to Russia despite Chamberblow's starting the policy of appeasement. He defended his actions by saying he had made "Peace in air time."[203]

Mussoliny, the dominant fascist of France, sought to form a state of the middle class: small businesses, farmers, and landowners. He led his army in a major march against Russia.[204] Fascists wanted control over Italy, Greece, and Britain. Then Mussoliny burst upon the Italian scene with a champagne of force.[205]

Mussoliny burst upon the Italian scene
with a champagne of force

In World War I, 700,000 Italian men had died. The war had cost the government 148 lire, more than a year's expenses. Political unrest and stalemate resulted. Mussoliny and his party tried to win seats in the legislature, but couldn't. The Fascists were anti-Nazi in ideology.

---

[203] Meaning on radio transmission time, direct from station NKVD from Chicovolk.

[204] Mussoliny's frequent invasions (France, Russia, Ethiopia, Greece) gave rise to the new expression of surprise, "What the Duce!" among European diplomats.

[205] Mussoliny himself drank far too much of this potent beverage, which led to his death in 1943.

Once Mussoliny had one of his opponents ride in a car with him. Needless to say, the man ended up dead. He used assassinations and firing squads. He shot and killed more people than Hitler or Stalin.

Communism taught that one should go out and kill a certain mass of people, whereas Fascism taught to go out and kill certain people, all the time. The Communists, led by dictator Lenin Stalin, were anti-Marxist in ideology. Stalin was elected in the Communist party government which gave him access to the party as a whole. This rule gave him much room to play with when setting up government totalitarianism.

Stalin was not a very polite person, although very earnest in his endeavors. He and his foreign minister, Vyochester Molonich, made speeches declaring the Western democracies as enemies. Russia and Britain made an accord (not a treaty) called the Triple Entente.

If anyone spoke against Stalin or was suspected of such a thing, he could be exiled or killed or both.[206] Stalin had a secret police called the Chico, and his army was called the Red Army or Bolshavics, sometimes known as the Red Shirts. The Communists had a red flag which stood for courage and a symbol of a cycle and a hammer (which meant they could crush or cut down any nation).

During World War II, some of the Soviet Union's women pilots were known as night whiches. Stalin employed specialists such as Werner von Brana, a rocket specialist, to keep the Soviets ahead. Soon the Soviets gained control of Poland, Yugoslavia, Checkoslovakia, Romania, Hungry, Bulvaria, and the Balklands.

All of these dictators had adolescent mind sets, while even the tsars were made to be Russian heroes.

Stalin strengthened the S.S. police and imprisoned many people. Like Mussoliny and Hitler, he used some common methods to rise to power by crushing all opponents, making massive arrests, and massive killings of children's regimes. The Communists used newspapers and pamphlets to spread ideals and gain support. Stalin used violence by sending people to forced labor camps in Siberia. The Communists would totally kill anyone who got in their way.

---

[206] Customarily, one was exiled before being killed, or, as the popular expression had it, "Put on ice."

25

The V-1 Rocket Could Be Shouted Down

World War II was the first world war that actually could use that name. The main reason for the war was the assassination of the Archduke of Spain in June of 1948 and the hostility between the European nations over past wars. William Randolph Hearst took the heir of the throne. The Duchess was then killed as well.

On May 1, 1939, the war began as Hitler had his troops invade Poland in the demilitarized Rhineland with his thunderous attack called the Blitzkrieg. This led Britain and France to declare war on Germany. The war involved many nations all around the world, including Asia, Africa, both the Artics, and countries like Australia and India.

Italy later joined the Allies after Sicily surrendered to the Hawaiians.[207] The splitzkrieg was a phony war; some called it a quiet war.

The United States entered World War II on June 4, 1938, and again in December 1949 after the Japanese twice bombed the U.S. Pacific Navel Fleet stationed in Pearl Harbor, Hawaii—a day that would live in emphemy, Truman said.

When the Japanese attacked, the Americans and Japanese were still talking, led by Emperor Tojo. In the war, the United States used island hooping in the Pacific.[208] Its bombs were more targeted and the Japanese

---

[207] The Hawaiians then put Sicily on the Dole, which enabled them to have pineapple on their pizzas.

[208] This popular Hawaiian pastime became a great favorite among the sailors of the Navel Fleet and later in the '50s, quite a fad in the US as hula hoops sold like candy among the Navel Set.

army bases and oil refiners were destroyed. The U.S. tried to establish bases on islands that were occupied by the Japanese. Then the U.S. fought the great navel battle of Midway in 1942, which put a damper on the Japs' spirits.

In WWII the German Mesheschitz, the Japanese Stukas, the British Spitfires, and the U.S. Semerschmidts were fast, maneuverable, and state-of-the-art flying machines. Then the British invented the Hurricane and the Starfire. The Messerschmidt was the first jet fighter in 1944. It was faster than the German Athera. They could carry canons and more guns as well. The Spitfire was known for its rapid climbing and the Hurricane planes were driven by komakaze pilots.[209]

The United States used island hooping in the Pacific

During the war, the British bombed basically just areas of Germany to lower morals. Saturation bombing was done where they would bomb certain buildings or give the people something to worry about. The Superfortress bombers delivered bombs right on their front doorstep.[210]

---

[209] The Hurricanes were so fast that sometimes pilots fainted or went into comas (hence the nickname "komakaze") from the excessive G's of a rapid descent.

[210] These mail-order bombs were called "smart bombs"; they could be ordered in various sizes and colors.

Places like Norway, Austria, Czechekoslovilia, and Poland were bombarbed with Hitler's passion. The Nazis invaded many countries such as the United States and London.

In the Pacific Theatre, the poor Japanese Komakazi pilots were guided missiles who flew their planes into boats, buildings, whatever. Needless to say, the plane, the building, the Jap, and anyone else in the way was blown away. By D-Day, nearly every major European city was leveled.

The Blitscreek or lightning strike of the Germans was almost a type of mass slaughtering. Hitler bombed London like some students bomb quizzes. Bombs were dropped wherever they fell. But the bombings of London caused much family strife as Moms and Dads had to send their children away to Canada, thus forming the story of Narnia. Russia invented radar to detect waves of German bombers.

The V-1 and V-2 rockets were made by the United States. The V-1 rocket was very slow, so slow that it could be shouted down.[211] Also in the air were the first guided missiles, the German VI and VII. The Germans attacked London from the air for two months straight, killing some 15,000. This project was called the Luftwaffe.

Submarine warships such as the British Dreadnoughts introduced almost global capabilities of warfare on the open seas, allowing forces to strike more effectively at supply lines. New battleships that were moving bases provided constant fuel and supplies for planes and fighters. Then battleships were large enough to land a plane to stock up for another run.[212] The aircraft carrier was something really big. This was really good because it not only had the navel part, but also the airplanes as well.

During WWII, the U.S. produced one car and a jeep every two minutes and a Liberty Ship every ten minutes. It made battle ships every hour. Women were definitely doing a good job in the work force. Elizabeth II, Queen Victoria's daughter, was one of the women who helped in a voluntary fight for peace on the home front.[213] Submarines were improved; they could now carry bigger torrepedas. Tanks were also more durable and able to endure more.

One of the new inventions of WWII was the atomic bomb which was

---

[211] This really happened in 1940 when the raucous debates among MPs in the Commons brought a V-1 rocket crashing through the roof of Parliament, barely missing Big Ben.

[212] Battleships then had collapsible smokestacks which, when retracted, cleared a sizable amount of deck space for the Semeschmidts and Spitfires to land.

[213] Princess Elizabeth drove a jeep and talked about changing spark plugs at dinners in Windsor Castle, to the distraction of her mother and father.

first used in Mexico and then in Hermin and Wiksuk in Japan in October 1942, making a new nuclear age. The United States also landed the atomic bomb on Japan at Hiroshima in December 1945, killing about 70,000, and then dropped it on the Germans at Nagasaki.[214]

Because of the fear of Japanese patriotism and dedication, President Harry S. Roosevelt ordered these attacks to discourage the Japanese and prevent a war from taking place involving Japan and the United States. He stated he wanted to end the war before it could start.

WWII also helped advance women's roles during the nineteenth century by enabling them to get more jobs in countries such as Britain and the Soviet Union.[215] Women became part of the entertainment world. Marlene Dixon and Shirley Temple would enhance the spirits of those fighting in the war and the world through their dancing and singing.

The total number of wounded, missing in action, or killed, including military and civilians during WWII, was 51,222,000,000. After the war, European countries no longer had the say as to what they wanted, for they now had the two supper powers.

When the Cold War started, Europe had front row tickets. The Cold War began due to amnesty and resentment between the U.S. and the Soviet Union.

The Soviets and America went to war and the winner would take all. Instead of starting everything like it always had, Europe waited nervously for something to start. Propaganada was at an all-time high at this time. The Cold War was a rhetoric war with tactful actions.[216]

The Truman Doctrine, which was written by Harry S. Truman, was to avoid Soviet expansion into the eastern Mediterranean. After WWII, Russia had possessed the west side of Berlin, and that was OK. Britain, France, and the U.S. decided to join their zones to form Western Europe.

The Iron Curtain was a slogan popular when the Russians were trying to starve West Germany. The Soviets imposed what was known as the Birlian Blockade and the Allies countered with the Birlian Airlift, or

---

[214] The limited number of atomic bombs available in 1945 and the great expense in producing them forced the U.S. to restrict its bombing to Mexico, Japan, and Germany.

[215] Remember that the time warp phenomenon accounts for this back-to-the-future influence on women's roles in the nineteenth century.

[216] One has only to recall the rhetoric surrounding the Berlin Blockade, the Korean War, and the Cuban Missile Crisis to regret that such tactful diplomacy no longer exists.

"Operator Vitals," of 1948-49. This caused the Berlian War, which lasted until 1989.

Military alliances also popped out of the Cold War. NATO, made in 1949, stood for the Nation Arms Treaty Organization. It consisted of the United States, Britain, France, Canada, Belgium, Iceland, Poland, Greece, Hungary, Italy, and many other nations who promised to go to war with one another if anyone was attacked by Communist forces.

Then CENTO and SENTO were formed with the U.S. in the 1950s as well which linked America with 42 states on its side. From 1950 to 1953 was the Korean War, during which General McArthur told North Koreans to go back to the border.

The Russian premier Khrushchev sometimes acted like a buffoon. The Soviets during the Cold War also launched IBMs and later the satellite Sputnik, which intensified the tension between the US and USSR. In the late 1950s and 1960s, Communist movement started to happen around Vietnam, where Hoshimin and his army attacked the democratic side of Vietnam. Such events helped nations realize they must piecefully coexist.

The V-1 rocket was so slow that it could be shouted down

26

The KKK Is an
Especially Black Period

In the 1940s and 1950s cultural setting, Mr. Ed, the talking horse, was inducted into movies Hall of Fame. During the same era, the cities of Kalamazoo and Chattanooga could thank Tex Beneke for putting them on the map. Then Carmen Miranda, a man from Brazil, introduced ballet dancing and revolutionized dance steps. Ben Hur wrote *How Green Was My Valley* and then started a television program about the tamed bear (Gentle Ben) before making a movie about a man who raced horses and buggies.[217]

During the 1960s, Elvis Presley sang songs about bad relationships. Then on November 22, 1963, John F. Kennedy was assassinated by Oswald, who was later killed by Polk.[218] Under the lunch law, the KKK made Blacks fear lynchings, abuse, death and destruction. The KKK is an especially black period in this era. Martin Luther King was a black equal rights leader whose main phrase was, "I got a dream."

The hippie counter-culture talked about the nonproliferation treaty in 1968, which developed the peace sign of the hippies. The Beatles invaded the United States with Beatlemania—screaming girls, paintings, etc., were a common sight at their appearances. The clothes of people who listened to rock and roll were decadent and comfortable.

---

[217] Ben Hur was one of Hollywood's best actors, equally at home in the coal mines of Wales, the Florida Everglades, the Red Sea's parting, and the hippodromes of Rome. His equal is seldom seen today.

[218] This idea of a back-to-the-future Polk/JFK connection opens the way for yet another conspiracy theory.

In literature, Samuel Beckett was one of the more outstanding Absurdists who wrote *Waiting for Godot*, a play wherein two men sit and wait for apparently nothing. Becket keeps his audience in suspense, not by making them wonder what will happen next, but by making them wonder what the hell is going on right now.

In art, Pollock's painting was called "Lavendermist," which reflected the moods and emotions of the people at that time, which were in a frenzy. Another type of art was expressed by Andy Warsaw called "pop art." He had a different style in which he expressed people's feelings and moods by taking a picture of a famous movie star, such as Maryland Monroe, along with the label off of a Campbell's soup can, and fusing them together with a stamp to form social icons and show the ever-changing emotions of the people in that time.

Then all of a sudden we were in the 1970s. Things began to ease up over in Panama, which was a town in Colombo, where they were trying to make an isthmus. Then the Vietcong War started with Koreans and no one won for eight years.

Ben Hur made a movie about a man who raced horses and buggies

And In Conclusion...

All of these contributions have been great, but the greatest contribution of all was that they lived, they reproduced, and here we are today, to hopefully carry on the human race.

About the Author

Despite writing the fractured footnotes in this book, Brian Strayer actually has three bona fide degrees in history from Southern Adventist University (B.A., 1973), Andrews University (M.A., 1974), and the University of Iowa (Ph.D., 1987). He has taught history to junior high, high school, college, and graduate school students. He is the author of eight books and scores of articles on such obscure groups as the Huguenots, Jansenists, and Adventists and such grisly topics as the prisons, police, and methods of torture and execution in Old Regime France.

Professor Strayer delights in studying the "twilight zone" in which past and present overlap—a zone in which you can never be certain whether you are on Planet Earth, Middle-Earth, Narnia, Perelandra, or with Alice in Wonderland. Those who read this delightful collection of student bloopers will find that history, herstory, and hysteria often coexist and that the past is always present!

Image Credits

(Seriously, these are the real thing. Really.)

Frontispiece. Detail of mosaic from the House of the Faun, Pompeii; Roman, 1st century.

p. 5. Celestial chart of classical constellations. Copperplate engraving from *Atlas Coelestis seu Harmonia Macrocosmica*; Dutch, 1708.

p. 6. The Pyramids. English print, ca. 1790.

p. 8. "Destruction of the Athenian Army in Sicily." Engraving, H. Vogel, 19th century.

p. 9. Greek orders of architecture. Engraving from the *Encyclopédie*; Paris, 1751-72.

p. 10. Women at leisure. Drawing from an ancient Roman relief.

p. 15. "The Soldier." Woodcut from the "Dance of Death" series, Hans Holbein; German, 16th century.

p. 16. "Orpheus in front of Pluto and Proserpina" (detail). Engraving, Virgil Solis, for Ovid's *Metamorphoses*; 16th century.

p. 18. Book illustration depicting classical history, unknown; 19th century.

p. 20. Four-wheeled carroballista drawn by armored horses. Engraving from the war-machine catalog *De Rebus Bellicis*, 1552.

p. 23. "Christians Flung To The Wild Beasts." Illustration from *A Popular History of Rome*; London, 1886.

p. 26. Germanic warriors and kings of the Dark Ages (detail). Engraving, German, 19th century.

p. 30. Murder of Thomas á Becket. Woodcut from Caxton's *The Golden Legend*, 1484-85.

p. 31. Knight on horseback. Woodcut from *Fierabras*; Lyon, ca. 1485.

p. 34. Protestants and Jews accused by the Inquisition of heresy and witchcraft. Woodcut; Nuremberg, 1493.

p. 37. Martin Luther's triumph over the monkish devil (detail). Woodcut, from Mattheus Gnidius's *Dialogi*, a Reform pamphlet against Papists; Germany, 1521.

p. 39. The Papist Devil, *"Ego sum Papa"* (I am the Pope). Woodcut from a Reformation handbill against Pope Alexander VI; Paris, late 15th century.

p. 44. Allegorical representation of Death. Woodcut, Nicolas le Rouge, *Le grand kalendrier ou compost des Bergiers*; Troyes, 1496.

p. 48. Battle between cranes and pygmies. Woodcut from the *Nuremberg Chronicle*; German, 1493.

p. 51. "Romans During the Decadence." Engraving, from original painting by Thomas Couture; French, 1847.

p. 53. The pope selling indulgences. Woodcut, studio of Lucas Cranach the Elder, from Philipp Melancthon, *Passional Christi und Antichristi*; Berlin, 1521.

p. 57. "Elizabetha Regina." Engraving, from *A Booke of Christian Prayers*; London, 1569.

p. 58. Witches' brew. Woodcut from Abraham Saur's *Ein Kurtze Treue Warnung* (A Short, True Warning); Frankfurt, 1582.

p. 61. "The Hurricane" (frontispiece to *The Tempest*). From *The Works of Mr. William Shakespear: Adorn'd with cuts*, Nicholas Rowe, ed.; London, 1709.

p. 64. Execution of Charles I. Woodcut; English, 17th century.

p. 65. Figures from funeral procession of the Duke of Albemarle (detail). Engraving; English, 1670.

p. 67. The lute player. Etching, Abraham Bosse; English, ca. 1640.

p. 69. Execution of the Huguenot conspirators at Amboise, 1560 (detail). Engraving, after Jacques Tortorel and Jean Perrissin; French, 1569-1570.

p. 71. Louis XIV in costume as Apollo for the "Ballet Royal de la Nuit." Engraving, Henri de Gissey; French, 1653.

p. 73. "Bad War." Engraving, Hans Holbein the Younger; German, 16th century.

p. 76. "The Imperial Jack-in-the-Box." Originally published in *Punch*, 1893. From *Punch Cartoons of the Great War*; New York, 1915.

p. 78. Skeleton with skull. Woodcut, from Andreas Vesalius, *De humani corporis fabrica libri septem* (On the fabric of the human body in seven books); Swiss, 1543.

p. 80. Satirical cartoon depicting the Third Estate (a peasant) supporting the First and Second Estates (clergy and nobility). French, 1780s.

p. 82. Illustration of Act I, Scene 2 from the drama *Kabale und Liebe* (Intrigue and Love) by Friedrich Schiller, 1784. Copper engraving, Daniel Chodowiecki; German, 1786.

p. 86. "Beer Street and Gin Lane" (detail). Engraving, William Hogarth; English, 1751.

p. 88. Laundresses. Source unknown, 18th-19th century.

p. 91. The Boston Tea Party. Engraving; American, 18th-19th century.

p. 92. "The Battle of Bunker Hill." Engraving, from original painting by John Trumbull; American, mid 19th century.

p. 94. "Q Quartered It." Wood engraving, from Kate Greenaway, *A Apple Pie*; London, 1886.

p. 95. "G Got It." Wood engraving, illustration from *A Apple Pie*.

p. 97. Execution of Louis XVI. Engraving; French, 1793.

p. 98. "La jolie sans-culotte en armes" (The pretty sans-culotte armed, with the sans-culotte of August 10th). Redrawn and merged 19th-century version of two early 1790s prints, for Augustin Challamel, *Histoire-musée de la république Française, depuis l'assemblée des notables*; Paris, 1842.

p. 100. "N Nodded For It." Wood engraving, illustration from *A Apple Pie*.

p. 103. "Trans-Atlantic Low-Altitude Train." Wood engraving, satirical cartoon published in *Barker's 1893 Illustrated Almanac*; American, 1893-94.

p. 105. "Bucks of the First Head." Engraving, from original late-18th-century watercolor by Thomas Rowlandson, in A. Hamilton Gibbs, *Rowlandson's Oxford*; London, 1911.

p. 107. Ballad singer. English illustration, mid 19th century.

p. 110. Combat between Romans and Britons. Illustration, William Harvey, from Thomas Miller, *History of the Anglo-Saxons*; London, 1850.

p. 113. "Christmas Dinner." Illustration, Robert Seymour, from *The Book of Christmas*; English, 1836.

p. 116. "The Gorilla and the Leopard." Illustration from Alfred Edmund Brehm, *Life of Animals: a complete natural history for popular home instruction and for the use of schools. Volume I: Mammalia*; Chicago, 1895.

p. 119. "If a body meet a body comin' through the rye." Cartoon satirizing the temperance movement; American, 1874.

p. 121. The Flapper. Ink cartoon; American, 1920s.

p. 124. Pursuit of the last Communard insurgents through Père-Lachaise cemetery, May 27, 1871. Engraving, *Le Monde Illustré*, N° 741; Paris, 1871.

p. 125. Geometry and angles. Engraving from the *Encyclopédie*; Paris, 1751-72.

p. 127. Boys fighting in the schoolyard. Unknown, probably American, late 19th century.

p. 128. "The breaking of the spell: Steinbach, January 3, 1915." Engraving, originally published in *Punch*, 1915. From *Punch Cartoons of the Great War*.

p. 130. "The Teutonising of Turkey." Engraving, originally published in *Punch*, 1910. From *Punch Cartoons of the Great War*.

p. 135. Little girl with a hoop. Ink drawing for advertisement or schoolbook; American, 1940s-50s.

With thanks to:

Wikipedia.org

Gutenberg.org

www.godecookery.com/clipart/clart.htm

www.godecookery.com/macabre/macabre.htm

www.wpclipart.com

www.fromoldbooks.org/

www.biodiversitylibrary.org/

www.karenswhimsy.com/

www.thegraphicsfairy.com/

Uncredited pictures are stock, public domain images of unknown source.

HISTORY AND HISTORICAL FICTION FROM SPYDERWORT PRESS:

CHILDREN'S HISTORICAL FICTION (AGES 9-12)

Hannah's Hessian
Deborah Remembers
The Grist Mill Secret
The Spinning Wheel Secret
Susanna's Candlestick
Lillie V. Albrecht

HISTORICAL FICTION

The Executioner's Heir:
A Novel of Eighteenth-Century France
Susanne Alleyn

HISTORICAL NONFICTION

Medieval Underpants and Other Blunders
Susanne Alleyn

A Tale of Two Cities: A Reader's Companion
(The Annotated *A Tale of Two Cities*)
Susanne Alleyn

ℒ ☯

37520993R00090

Made in the USA
Lexington, KY
05 December 2014